STACEY JONES
Kiwi Warrior

STACEY
JONES
Kiwi Warrior

with Richard Becht

Hodder Moa

National Library of New Zealand Cataloguing-in-Publication Data
Becht, Richard.
Stacey Jones : Kiwi Warrior / Richard Becht.
ISBN 1-86971-051-7
1. Jones, Stacey, 1976- 2. Vodafone Warriors (Rugby team)
3. Kiwis (Rugby League team) 4. Rugby League football players
—New Zealand—Biography. 5. Rugby League football—
Australia. 6. Rugby League football—New Zealand. I. Title.
796.3338092—dc 22

A Hodder Moa Book
Published in 2005 by Hachette Livre NZ Ltd
4 Whetu Place, Mairangi Bay
Auckland, New Zealand

Designed and produced by Hachette Livre NZ Ltd
Printed by Business Printing Group Ltd, Auckland

Front and back cover photography: Photosport

To Rachelle, Chellcey and Waiana

Mum and Dad

Trish and Dave.

I can't say enough.

Contents

About the writer

Richard Becht has been a journalist for more than 30 years, working in print, television, radio and public relations. Born in 1955 and raised in Te Aroha, most of his career has centred on sport.

Major overseas assignments have included Olympic and Commonwealth Games, the Rugby World Cup, the America's Cup and soccer's 1982 World Cup finals.

Among numerous books he has written are titles on rugby league legends Graham Lowe, Gary Freeman, Dean Bell and Tawera Nikau, cricketing great Sir Richard Hadlee and All Black star Carlos Spencer. He has also produced a nostalgic work on motor racing heroes Bruce McLaren, Denny Hulme and Chris Amon, another on the creation of the Warriors and publications covering New Zealand's 1995, 2000 and 2003 America's Cup campaigns.

In 2004, he joined the Vodafone Warriors as media and communications manager.

Acknowledgements

I owe so much, to so many people. Thanks to:
- Jason and Jamie, for toughening up your little brother.
- Nan and Papa and Nana and Pop, for always being there.
- Rachelle's mum Roberta and other family and friends, for your constant support.
- Awen, Tash and family, for a precious friendship.
- Eric Watson, special thanks for the Foreword.
- Peter Leitch (the Mad Butcher) and family. You've always been there to help.
- Gordon Gibbons, Peter Kean and the team at Lion Breweries — long live Lion Red.
- Clark Todd and the team at Nike, for always making my boots fit perfectly.
- Alan Kirby and the team at North Harbour Ford. Great wheels to get me to and from training.
- Terry Baker, nothing was ever too much.
- Peter Brown, for everything you've done for me.
- All coaches, players and football staff, for a lifetime of memories.
- Warren Adler and Hachette Livre NZ, always so professional.
- Richard Becht, for putting all this together.

Stacey Jones
September 2005

Special thanks to Stacey for the chance to work with him.

Thanks also to Warren Adler and Hachette Livre NZ for their commitment to a project that ran to a tight deadline.

Several publications were valuable sources of information, principally various editions of the *New Zealand Rugby League Annual*.

Thanks also to Andrew Cornaga of Photosport who provided the majority of the images in the book.

Richard Becht
September 2005

Foreword

When Cullen Sports took over the Vodafone Warriors in late 2000, there was a long list of priorities. The most urgent was the need to ensure we secured Stacey Jones for as long as possible.

In a business sense he was the club's primary asset, the player who meant the most to the team, to the club as a whole and to the sporting community at large. In reality he *was* the Warriors.

To make the organisation viable, it was clear we had to retain Stacey so we could begin the task of re-launching and rebuilding a club that had so much potential. He was a valuable link with the past but he was very much the cure for the future.

Now, five years later, Stacey has asked me to write the foreword for his book, his story of a lifetime in rugby league. I'm enormously privileged to do so. It's sad on the one hand that he has finished with the club he started his career with, but it's also exciting for Stacey and his family that a new adventure lies ahead.

Far more important to us and to all New Zealanders is the contribution he has made to the Warriors and to rugby league since he started out in 1995. In his time he has been as recognisable and as popular as any sporting figure in this country, yet, while being a gifted athlete, he has remained so humble; it's that combination of excellence and humility that has won him such admiration.

That admiration was palpable when the Warriors held their annual awards dinner shortly after their 2005 season finished. It was a night to acknowledge the year's achievers but it was also a night to mark Stacey's contribution and to thank him for it. It was a moving experience for everyone in the room as we watched images that exposed Stacey Jones the man more than Stacey Jones the footballer. It served to reinforce that he really has been the ideal sporting package, the like of which we may never see again.

New Zealand sport has been blessed to have him and the Warriors have been the luckiest of all. He'll be missed at the club but we'll never forget how much he gave of himself, how even in the greatest adversity he displayed levels of loyalty too rarely seen.

The words 'great' and 'legend' are liberally used at times but they'll always apply to Stacey Jones, a great New Zealander and a sporting legend.

Eric Watson
Auckland, September 2005

The first farewell

For 11 years, Stacey Jones ran a rugby league race made up of little else but firsts with the Warriors. First to 100, 150 and 200 first-grade games, first to 50 tries, 500 points and first to anything else that might register.

Until one week in 2005, that was. Suddenly it was about lasts, most of them revolving around match day itself. On that day — 20 August — Stacey Jones was going about his business trying not to think about the past or the end. As he'd always done, he wanted to keep this as basic as he possibly could, to stay in the moment.

There was no way, though, that this would ever be just another match. That's because history will always recall the 237th appearance of his National Rugby League career as his last for the Warriors at home, his last in front of family, friends and fans at Ericsson Stadium, his last running out onto his field of dreams with the gladiators he was so used to going into battle with.

Across 11 seasons, he'd been cruising back and forth between home and the industrial suburb of Penrose more times than he knew. On a conservative count, he must have made the round trip about 200 times a year, somewhere around 2200 times in all totalling more than

50,000 kilometres in distance covered. It would be asking too much to work out how many kilometres he'd clocked up on the training field from 1995 to 2005, but the journey that always meant the most was the one he made from dressing room to full noise out in the middle at his home ground. Everything else was incidental.

After two Winfield Cup appearances on the road, he first experienced the hometown thrill as a top-grade player against the then-named Sydney Tigers on 4 June 1995. It happened to be a tryscoring and match-winning exercise as well but there had never been a game to match his 118th NRL outing at Ericsson Stadium.

Shortly after 7.30 on the evening of 20 August, Stacey William Jones ran onto the stadium — his stadium — without his usual support network around him. His team-mates held back, according their illustrious colleague the honour he deserved on this night. Leading him out were two youngsters wearing his junior club colours of Ponsonby and Point Chevalier, the latter worn by Jones' niece Laishon. For a few, almost vulnerable, moments the 29-year-old former Kiwi captain might have felt somehow alone despite being surrounded by thousands of friendly, even adoring, faces. They were blasting out a vocal salute that went only part way to expressing how much this little man had meant to so many New Zealanders.

Soon enough the man who has done as much for the number seven as Jonah Lomu did for the numeral 11 during his rugby union career was reunited with his brothers, back in the fray doing what has always come naturally to him. That he should be doing so against the quite extraordinary Newcastle No 7, Andrew Johns, served only to give this goodbye turn added appeal.

Jones and Johns don't have too much time left in the game but, when they finish, rugby league and sport in the widest sense in this part of the world will always recall them as two of the most wondrous footballing talents to spoil anyone who watches sport. On this night they lined up against each other boasting individual records of almost freakish similarity — New Zealand's Jones man with 236 games and 74 tries, Australia's Johns bloke with 222 matches and 70 tries.

In footballing expression they have always been slightly different, though, and on 20 August 2005, the 17,356 spectators at the ground and hundreds of thousands watching screens on both sides of the Tasman would see it for themselves one last time . . .

There it goes again — another last, just as it had been throughout the previous week and especially in the final 90 minutes or so before making his dramatic final Warriors entrance.

This last act hadn't just been a week, let alone 90 minutes, in the making. Indeed it was the manifestation of what might have come about in a much gloomier manner had Jones followed through with his wish to leave when life as a Warrior turned sour in 2004. He'd been turned around, though, and in this season and during this week he knew he'd done so — or had been convinced to do so — for all the right reasons.

The first public hint Jones was definitely into a countdown to goodbye had actually appeared on the eve of the 2005 NRL season starting — not that many people picked up on the development at the time. It emerged as the Vodafone Warriors' season was launched with the Captain's Lunch in Ericsson Stadium's new East Stand, a corporate occasion featuring new captain Steve Price as the keynote speaker. Expectation hung in the air as the players and coaching staff eyed the start of their campaign after weeks of slogging in the sun; in his eloquent way, Price talked of his personal sense of anticipation about his new challenge after 11 seasons with the Bulldogs. There was no question he impressed the 300 guests there who, in turn, were excited to see the upgraded Ericsson Stadium looking infinitely better than it ever had.

Coincidentally, the previous day had marked the 10th anniversary of the Warriors' introduction to what was then the Winfield Cup and had now evolved into the National Rugby League. Jones was there that original night — 10 March 1995 — as a reserve grader, goggle-eyed at what unfolded.

This was a poignant time then to acknowledge history, to celebrate it and to warm to what was in store in season 2005. With the past, present and future in mind it meant the focal point of the afternoon wasn't necessarily Price or his team-mates en masse. It proved to be Stacey Jones, for he alone covered every year of the club's existence from gestation, to *enfant terrible* and brooding adolescent before the adult form took shape, replete with all its foibles.

Vodafone Warriors CEO Mick Watson, also destined to move on at the end of the season, began proceedings by steering clear of any predictions about the coming campaign: 'All I will say is that at 2 p.m. on Sunday we'll step onto the rollercoaster — so strap yourselves in, hang on, here we go.' In his address he also harked back to the club's first three successful years under Cullen Sports' ownership before 2004's disappointments. 'Consecutive finals . . . minor premiership . . . grand finalists . . . a successful, profitable brand,' he said. 'Vince Lombardi once said: "Winning is not a sometime thing, it's an all-the-time thing." We've learnt our lesson the hard way.'

Decked out in their sharp new RJB-designed suits, Watson asked the 17 players selected for the season-opener against Manly to join him at the front of the stage.

'Eight months ago I asked the players why they started playing rugby league and what drives them. Awen Guttenbeil's response was: "I play because I love the challenge. I started because it was a way of life for my family. When I play I represent my family. We all live the same dream and I'm proud to be the one they can do that through."

'Everybody in this club has worked very hard to rebuild our platform, to rebuild it for today and to create a legacy for others to follow and be proud of. We've selected these 17 Vodafone Warriors to place our trust in, for them to be the custodians of all our hopes and dreams — for the fans, sponsors and everyone associated with the club. We've selected them because they've worked hard and they deserve our trust.'

One of the 17 was, of course, Stacey Jones and appropriately and intentionally Watson used the occasion to mark Jones' contribution to the club in a special way, telling the 300 guests: 'The club has a fragmented history but in every club there is one player who comes across as a once-in-a-lifetime player, someone who has made a contribution far more significant than any other.' He was able to reel off a succession of Jones' club achievements — most games (215), most points (507), most tries (70), most field goals (11) . . . 'The list just goes on and on,' he said, before inducting the champion halfback as a Vodafone Warriors' life member.

'This is a great honour,' said Jones. 'This club has been such a huge part of my life. I feel really honoured to receive this award.' Price, who had himself been made a Bulldogs life member, added: 'What the club has done for Stacey today is massive. The history of a club is so important and I think it's a huge pat on the back that this has been done.'

It was quite a pat and one few New Zealanders could have deserved more in their chosen sport. What it implicitly said, though, was that Jones was about to start his last season as a Warrior; there had also been mention of a testimonial for him later in the season, another pointer towards him taking his rugby league talents to another corner of the globe after the 2005 season.

When that official announcement duly came not too many weeks later it didn't sit well with the sporting public, even though it did with the man himself. Try as he might, there was a limited buy-in when he said he was ready to go, that it was time to move on for both lifestyle and football reasons.

It meant season 2005 became one long farewell. Jones treated it that way and wanted to make the most of it, but not until his days as a Warrior were numbered did supporters truly begin to appreciate the one constant at Ericsson Stadium was down to his last few appearances in front of them. In four of his last five home games there was glory against Brisbane in late June, utter heartbreak when the Bulldogs came to town, a polished performance in beating Canberra and a soft showing against Parramatta. And then it came down to the last week before his last home game . . .

This, for Jones, was the week of weeks before the night of Knights. It came after the Warriors' season had been all but derailed by a 22–10 loss to the Storm in Melbourne. Defeat had left the club needing to win the last two matches against Newcastle and Manly and then hope for some cards to fall the right way.

With or without the right results, the Knights' visit was always going to coincide with a monster occasion. That much had been determined many weeks earlier when the club moved into overdrive to ensure this would be both a week and a night to remember. Whatever the state of the top eight race, Stacey's farewell was always the big selling point. Other legendary performers, such as Richard Hadlee, Jonah Lomu and more recently Andrew Mehrtens and Justin Marshall, have done so much for New Zealand sport but when their time was up they went almost quietly without any special fanfare. Not Stacey Jones, and that surely underlined his appeal as an achiever ordinary New Zealanders deeply admired; not just admired, but loved.

The indefatigable Peter Leitch launched himself into a titanic operation to organise the Stacey Jones Testimonial Lunch, as it was called. It was scheduled for 17 August and, remembering it was a midweek event with a decent ticket price per plate, it was nothing short of stunning that the show was sold out some five weeks before it took place. Not just sold out, but also with a waiting list. With minimum promotion, close to 900 people were squeezed into the Ellerslie Convention Centre for a lunch many were still talking about weeks later.

As sports occasions go, this was one for the ages.

The room wasn't just bursting with people; it was brimful with famous sporting names, too, naturally including the entire Vodafone Warriors squad, football department and management. Mick Watson began the speeches with a succinct tribute to Jones. NRL CEO David Gallop — who made a special trip from Sydney — offered an Australian view and New Zealand Rugby League's Selwyn Pearson, in his inimitable way, had his say. Prime Minister Helen Clark was another of the special guests and, with her long association with league, she recounted the times when she used to give out prizes galore to a young Stacey Jones. No one else seemed to get a look-in, she said. Through every speech the take-out was the same as Jones was recalled for his breathtaking ability but, at the same time, an astonishing humility which is not always characteristic of gifted athletes.

Later, in the first of a series of rapid-fire interviews, Warriors head coach Tony Kemp said: 'It will be a sad day for all of us when Stacey leaves the country. For as long as I have known him, Stacey has been an icon in New Zealand. If I could sum him up I'd put him alongside two great superstars we have in Jonah Lomu, who was outstanding in his area of sport, and Sunline, who was miles ahead of any other horse in this country. As far as I'm concerned, Stacey Jones is probably the best league player ever to come out of this place.'

In his role as MC, Peter Leitch moved on to Gene Ngamu, one of Jones' colleagues with the Kiwis and the Warriors, who related stories about his team-mate's great ability to misplace his dental plate. Once Jones found it in the bottom of a washing machine after it had been missing for a few days.

Kevin Campion, a fellow Warrior in 2001–02 but one of the coaching staff in 2005, has always had the highest opinion of Jones. 'It was just a pleasure playing with Stace,' he said. 'When I first got here it was like going back in time when I'd played with Alfie Langer. I think Stace had the same sort of influence on the game as Alfie did. The first thing I had to do was to earn Stacey's respect, as I did with Alfie at the Broncos. It took a while. In the first year here I played like a busted mug and it took a while to earn his respect. We had a great couple of years here and made the grand final in 2002, which was a wonderful experience for me and for the rest of New Zealand and, in particular, for Stace. I'd played in a few before but with Stace you could see it in his eyes when we ran out onto the field on grand final day. I followed him out and I still get shivers up the spine about it.'

That was the serious and sincere stuff, where all the right things were said about the man in focus. Jones was never going to have it so easy once his supposed mate Awen Guttenbeil was behind the microphone, though. He'd waited for this moment and he'd planned meticulously for it; the end result was a barrel of laughs at the star turn's expense in a speech that reinforced what a special talent Guttenbeil has as a performer:

Kia ora. Firstly, Helen, it's good to see you here . . . Stace, it's probably time to hit her up for that land we want up north, bro.

When I first met Stacey in 1989 we were both 13 years old. Stace was playing for Auckland and I was playing for Northland. It was a rugby league tournament and I vividly remember everybody talking about this great talent Stacey Jones, how much of an athlete he was — everybody but the guys from up north. We were all talking about this halfback from Auckland who was the only 13-year-old we'd seen with a beard. I'm serious. Stacey was physically mature for a young man. He wouldn't have been much smaller than he is now, maybe a little lighter but certainly not shorter. He was never going to be a basketballer.

The following season I moved to Auckland and linked up with Point Chev, which was Stacey's club. We had a pretty good run in the four years we played there. We lost two games and that was hugely due to Stace. Every other kid wanted to come to the club to play for us and win games. Because Stace was in the team that pretty much guaranteed that would happen.

From the age of 14 to 17 you certainly learn a lot on the field — and you learn a huge amount off the field. We experienced a few things and got up to a bit of mischief. For the first time we experienced girls but we can't talk about that because we're both married now. One thing we do enjoy is a beer and we developed a thirst for it throughout our Point Chev days. We'd go to the prize-giving after the game and six of us would rock off. The loser would have to catch the bus from Point Chev to K Road to get some flagons of beer, catch the bus back and we'd get drunk at the park. Stacey was often the man because he had a lot of facial hair and looked a lot older than 15 so he was guaranteed to get the flagons.

In those years I also discovered that Stacey was a bit of a prankster. One time I was staying at Stacey's and there was a social on at the club. I didn't have any gear, just my tracksuit, so I didn't really want to go but Stacey convinced me. He said he'd give me a pair of one of his brother's jeans. His brothers were both six foot so I thought: 'Yeah, that's cool.' We were walking down to the club and I said: 'Gee, Stace, these are a bit tight.' He said: 'No, they'll stretch by the time you get down there. They've just been in the drier.' Anyway, I walked into the social, looked back at Stace and he was pissing himself laughing and so was everyone else. I'd managed to fit into Stacey's jeans. They came down just to my calf and were rather tight, except in the bum. He's always had a fair bum on him has Jones.

Following our time at Point Chev I took off to play in Oz for a couple of years and came back to play against Stacey (and the Warriors) in 1995. I was playing for the Manly reserve grade side and we lost the game 48–0 and Stacey was the star of that game. Three times we've played against each other — the first was Northland against Auckland in the under 13s. If it wasn't for the touch judge disallowing my fourth try we would have won that one. Then there was the game at Ericsson in 1995 and we also played against each other at the World Cup later that year. Stacey was playing his first test for New Zealand and I was playing for Tonga. As a Tongan player, I was in a team that was going pretty well. We were leading by 12 points with about eight minutes to go and I was giving Jones a bit of cheek, as you do with mates. He ran the ball up, I managed to grab hold of him and tackle him and then I tried to pull his pants down, to down-trou him while he was playing the ball. He looked back not very impressed and I was laughing, thinking: 'Yeah, we've got you here mate.' Eight minutes later we walked off, losing by one point thanks to a Ridgey field goal.

So, as I say, Stacey has beaten me three times on the league field but off it we're also very competitive. Stacey loves a challenge and, whether it's golf, cricket, lawn bowls, fishing or even recipes for cooking, we'll compete. The ledger is Stacey's won three in the league stakes but he's my whipping boy in the rest.

In 1996 I moved back from Australia to link up with the Warriors and for 10 years we've played alongside each other, and our mateship has obviously been there from the start. Having the same goals and determination I guess was our common denominator and we've certainly hung out as much as we could.

On and off the field I have tremendous memories of special moments with Stace. One of them off the field that Stacey and I were talking about the other day was just before Super League started, I think. The Warriors played Canberra in Canberra and in those days you'd enjoy a few beers and almost drink through the night and the next day on the plane home . . . but certainly not now.

We got on the drink the day after that game. We had a meeting at Lachlan

Murdoch's mansion. He was heavily involved in the Super League thing so they got us together to talk about that. Stacey being Stacey had drunk right through the night and we were sitting around the pool having a few beers and Mal Meninga was there, too. Stacey got a bit of a scratch under his eye from the game and Mal said: 'Hey, Stace, what's that under your eye? What happened there?' Stace took a swig of his beer, hung the bottom lip as he does when he's drunk, and said: 'Yeah! Yeah! Well, what happened here, mate? What about these? What about these?' (Jones had pointed at his eyebrows, mocking Meninga's famously prominent growth.)

Stacey couldn't remember that and it took us a few days to convince him he had said it. The funny part was the next year when we went to play Canberra he was the first person off the bus. I'd never seen him run into the dressing room so fast, play the game and then be the first back on the bus. He avoided Mal for a couple of years there. He was a bit embarrassed.

On the field we've had plenty of special moments in our junior days and seeing Stacey achieve what he has, has certainly been a highlight for me. But one of the most rewarding moments was after we'd beaten the Sharks and finally realised we were going to the grand final (in 2002). As kids we'd talked about it but never really believed we would achieve it. There was a moment when we caught each other's eyes and embraced. That was one of the best moments of my life, being there with your best mate achieving what you'd always wanted to.

For the last three years I've been Stacey's room-mate. We knock around doing pretty much everything we can together and I thought that's why they made us roomies. I figured out, though, that when Jones has a few beers he needs a minder and, knowing him so well, I'm the only guy who knows how to get him home.

The funny thing is, when Stace has had a few beers he's sweet as. He'll get to 12, no worries, 13, sweet as, 13 and a half, beautiful, still talking sense — but 13 and a half beers and one sip? That's all it takes, that one sip and you know you're in for a hard night trying to get him home. Once you get him home, he won't get out of the car and walk to the door himself. He'll get you to take him in and say hello to Rachelle. Just like the smart kid does, so he doesn't get in trouble in front of his wife. He's done that many times to all the boys in the off-season. He even got Campo to sleep at his home once.

Lion Red . . . what a beautiful beer — Stacey loves it. It was great to see the boys at Lion honour Stacey by giving him his own beer. I was a little disappointed, guys. I went to the launch and I thought this beer was meant to reflect Stacey. For one, it was a long neck. If it was a true Stacey Jones beer it would have been a stubby. The other thing I thought, just to make it a true Stacey Jones beer, was the label. It's nice with all the stats on it but I would have made it out of fur, something a bit fluffy so that when you turned the bottle around and stroked it, it felt just like Stace. The last thing I would have done as a subtle touch would be to have one of the teeth missing on the bottle top just so those who know him know it's a true Stacey Jones vintage.

Another thing with Stace when he's had a few beers is that he likes to get up to dance. For someone who's so athletic with all the footballing talents in the world I think, just for a joke, God rubbed the old shoes with the I-can't-dance gene. It confirms to me that the rumours about the cheerleader weren't true because I don't think Jones would be able to pick up someone who does dancing for a profession.

Thirteen years ago Stacey met a young Samoan girl and here they are today — they've had two beautiful children and have another on the way. I'd like to take this time to pay tribute to Rachelle. All the support, guidance and encouragement you've given Stace has helped him become the man he is today. You need to be commended. I'd also like to thank you for giving the time and making the sacrifices you do to allow Stacey to do what he does with us. As part of the team, Stacey's always the first at training or the first one giving up his time for the rest of us, so thanks from all of us.

Also on that note, to Stacey's parents Rama and Billy, his grandparents who are here and the rest of the whanau who have travelled long distances to be here — be very proud of this young man, and be very proud that you helped to mould him into the person he is. Rugby league in New Zealand is certainly better for that.

From the boys, Stace, we're going to miss you. We've got a few weeks left yet and I'm sure once it's all done we'll get a chance to express what it means you leaving.

I just want to say thank you for making this game that I love so much more enjoyable with you being a team-mate.

Jones managed a bit of a riposte, saying Guttenbeil's stories had a few turns and twists in them. Revenge, it was clear, would be saved for another day. The lunch was monstrous for the little man and then the Warriors' regular weekly media session the following day was a case of more of the same. Unsurprisingly, most approaches were for Jones, to the point where he spent almost three hours solid meeting media requirements for television, radio and newspaper outlets. All week it was similar as everyone tried to grab a slice of his time.

There had been a festive feel from one day to the next but Kemp and the coaching staff were obviously more serious as they tailored training around one goal — doing it for Jones. The week and the match, Kemp told the players, was all about one man, only he needed Friday to effectively recover, to kick back and rest up for an extreme physical and emotional experience the following day. And then it came down to the last 90 minutes before his last NRL match at home . . .

For the 2200th time (or thereabouts), he headed to Ericsson Stadium, leaving home a little before 5.30 p.m. He had to be at the club earlier than usual to satisfy another media commitment; understandably he was the only choice for Sky Sport to speak to for its pre-recorded locker-room interview.

That out of the way, Jones went about his usual routine, indulging in activities in the gym designed to perk the players up ahead of combat. He waited his turn to be strapped — physiotherapist Jude Spiers needing to give him support for a left knee that had been bothering him plus more strapping for his left forearm, left thumb and left shoulder. Jones slipped on his Vodafone Warriors Puma playing kit, his battledress, and his trademark tiny Nike boots. As other players were being strapped or had a massage amid music pounding out of a ghetto blaster, Jones wandered about between the dressing room and the adjoining gym contemplating what lay ahead. He'd been involved in far more important matches in front of enormous crowds — most obviously the 2002 NRL grand final — but few had meant as much as this one.

Outside the confines of the dressing room and gym, Ericsson Stadium was awash with Stacey Jones in one shape or another. Videotape inserts were shown on the big screen looking back at his career, farewell banners were visible all around the stadium and, as a nice touch, there was a mini league game between the little man's two junior clubs, Ponsonby and Point Chevalier.

Jones was oblivious it to it all, waiting instead as the countdown began for the warm-up — 10 minutes, five minutes, two minutes, one minute. 'Okay, boys let's go!' Price gathered his troops, led them out of the gym, past fans shouting support and then through the tunnel to the No 2 field at Ericsson Stadium. Kemp, assistant coaches Ivan Cleary, Kevin Campion and Tony Iro plus other support staff put the players through their final pre-game jousting. Jones had done this 236 times before in his first-grade career but now No 237 had more edge to it than usual. This was the last time, positively the last time, he'd be doing this for a home match for his beloved club.

Timed to the second, the 30-minute warm-up finished, the players jogging back through the tunnel, back past the fans and into the dressing room to take their seats, awaiting their final instructions and a few final words from players who had something to say. Some players headed to the toilets, the distinctive sound of dry retching reverberating around the room. Jones grabbed a paper cup of Gatorade, swallowed a mouthful and threw the rest away. He was one of the first to take his seat but a few seconds later he was up again asking team doctor Chris Hanna for some eye drops (could it be to hide the tears?).

Now everyone was ready, attentive. The players sat in their usual circular formation, Kemp with them. Looking at no one in particular, he said: 'A lot of you young blokes are going to wonder what this is all about. Well, tonight when you're blowing through your arse, just look over at the little bloke who's out there with you and think about what you're doing for him — and what he has done for you. Because I'm telling you, tonight it's all about him. This is a special occasion.'

With that, Kemp was out of his seat going around the room to shake hands with his players. Still in his seat, Jones seized the chance to have his say: 'This is one of the most enjoyable years I've had at the club. I love you all. You're great blokes so let's go out and do it tonight. Do our jobs.'

These were as special as moments come for Jones. The players went around the room hugging each other, slapping each other on the back. For Jones, there was more meaning and feeling than ever this time. Clearly the eye drops hadn't stopped the tears welling up. He has never been a man to open up emotionally but he was undeniably affected now. The two-minute bell went: two minutes to go before the team must head out onto the field. And then it arrived — the last 80 minutes of his life as a Warriors player at Ericsson Stadium . . .

For 60 minutes the Warriors were commanding everywhere but on the scoreboard. Throughout the first half they were putting on one play after another in Newcastle's red zone, in the 0–30-metre area:

3' 00"   Jones tries to pierce Newcastle's goal-line defence with a grubber. It ricochets off legs and the Knights mop it up.

4' 00"   Jones finds grass as he pumps a long kick deep inside Newcastle's 20.

6' 00"   Another Jones kick finds space behind Newcastle's defensive line.

12' 00"   The master picks his spot and reels off a stunning 40/20 kick to give the Vodafone Warriors a repeat set close to Newcastle's line.

17' 00"   A brilliant set in possession takes the Warriors way downfield before Jones caps it with a precision bomb to Manu Vatuvei's right wing. He out-leaps his opposite, snaffles the ball and scores.

23' 00"   Newcastle spills the ball, toed through, and Simon Mannering hammers Dustin Cooper. Ball spills loose, Jones sweeps it up and scampers away for a try — until video ref Steve Nash disallows it.

And so it went on with the Warriors calling the tune but leading only 4–0 at halftime. It was a travesty and it became a tragedy when Jones was denied two more would-be tries in the second half — the first in the 54th minute when he was penalised for a double movement and yet again four minutes later when he was across once more only to have the try disallowed on an obstruction call against Awen Guttenbeil. This was Stacey Jones' night but, at the same time, it wasn't. The rugby league gods certainly weren't helping, or at least someone playing God wasn't. The first two instances ought to have produced legitimate four-pointers but for the finger of fate in the first instance and a hasty referee's call in the second.

One way or another, the Warriors might have been — should have been — at least 10–0 if not 16–0 ahead at halftime with Sione Faumuina also botching a try as he was launching himself across the line. That they weren't substantially ahead still wasn't seen as a setback. Kemp was calm at the break, telling the players: 'Stay in this. Don't change what you're doing. It will work.' Jones, too, had a say as he appreciated the vital importance of his last 40 minutes as an NRL player at home. 'Watch the ruck, boys. Watch the ruck,' he implored.

In the opening 22 minutes of the second half, not too much changed. The flow of the contest mirrored the first stanza, the Warriors with possession and position with Jones across the line twice — and denied by officialdom each time — while a searing Awen Guttenbeil break was set to yield a try only to be stymied when he failed to feed one of the support players he had on either side of him. Jones was feverishly involved in everything that was going on but, instead, it was to be Johns rather than Jones who played the most influential hand, making the key plays to arrange three tries in the space of five minutes to give the Knights what proved to be a match-winning lead.

The sense of deflation around the ground — and on the field — was almost measurable. The difference this night was people stayed rather than indulge in the customary Ericsson Stadium shuffle in the face of defeat. Try as Jones and his team-mates might, they couldn't find the formula to extract an escape to force a dramatic victory or even the possibility of golden-point extra time. That hurt Jones and it disappointed the crowd that his final act shouldn't be capped appropriately, but they still had far too much respect for their favourite player to desert him now. So they stayed and so they hailed this special footballer.

When the siren went to mark fulltime for not just a match but effectively a career, Jones wasn't able to escape. There were obligatory post-match television and radio interviews, a group put on a haka, Andrew Johns sought his adversary out to commiserate with him and pose for a priceless photo of two of the world's greatest No 7s together for the last time. Somewhere in there were Jones' daughters Chellcey and Waiana, decked out in their Stacey Jones T-shirts ready to do a lap of the ground with Dad. And so the man of the hour began a trek that was meant to be joyful and celebratory but now didn't have the same appeal after what had happened. The defeat on the final night hurt but not as much as the manner of it, not after Jones himself had crossed the line three times and missed out on every one.

As he went around the ground waving, trying to smile, Jones was followed some distance behind by the rest of his team-mates. The Newcastle players respectfully stayed out on the field and allowed Jones to walk in front of the Western Stand patrons before they walked off. The cheergirls remained as well and finally came the trip back to the dressing room, his Warriors buddies forming a guard of honour for Jones to walk through and then departing team-mate Iafeta Paleaaesina to follow. Jones was hurting but inside the dressing room he refused to let it show. 'Let's just keep our heads up. Let's have a good night tonight,' he pleaded.

No one quite knew what to say. This had turned into a funereal experience rather than a cheerful one. It was still a time to capture for posterity, though. Photographer Andrew Cornaga was ushered into the inner sanctum, various players and football staff lining up for a shot alongside Jones. He obliged and then did so again for a group photo with most of the players plus his daughters. It was all worth it.

The image that stood out was to come and Cornaga, always with an eye for the big shot, found it in the locker room. Jones, scissors in one hand, was cutting and ripping away his strapping from his shoulder, from his arm and his knee, looking a rather forlorn figure as he added the final punctuation mark to his time as a Vodafone Warriors player.

The photo would leave an indelible impression when it boomed out from all three Sunday papers the next day.

There was still more ahead. On this night of all nights, Jones was faced with another date with the media. Never too keen on media conferences, he showered, dressed in his suit and joined Kemp and Price for a walk back across the ground to the Western Stand, the stand which he'd run out from so many times before. Requests for photos and autographs flowed as he walked, each politely declined with: 'I'll do it when I come back.'

After walking through the bowels of the stand, the entourage entered a packed room understandably bursting with more reporters, photographers and television cameras than usual. It was meant to be Jones' night and it started that way as he was queried about his assessment of the night and especially the decisions that prevented him being awarded even one of his three would-be tries. 'It was a bit of a heartbreak. I thought one of them was a try. What can you say?' Jones said in a desperately disappointed but certainly not angry tone. That wouldn't have been him. He went on: 'That's the way it went and you can't do nothing about it. It was frustrating. We were dropping the ball, turning it over and when we got over the line it was disallowed.'

He tried gamely to mask his disappointment by stressing the high points of an intense week. 'It was a pretty busy week but it was really enjoyable. I thought the boys were ready to play. We wanted to win this one so badly. It was our last home game and we couldn't quite make it. Maybe tomorrow [the end] will sink in [for me]. I guess it has been coming. It is a little bit sad to go out on this note. I really enjoyed my time at this club and playing with the guys that have been here and under Kempy. I really enjoyed it. Even though we didn't go out the way we wanted to, it was great playing under Kempy.'

Kemp, too, wanted to say his piece about the champion player but soon enough he changed the tone of the conference by zeroing in on the no-try decisions, a move which seemed to make Jones and Price a little uncomfortable and one which would later cause some consternation — but no NRL breach notice — on both sides of the

Tasman. Kemp started by saying: 'I will remember this game for three things. One was Newcastle coming to town, and I've always got a soft spot for them. Another was seeing Joey Johns run around again and then there was seeing Stacey Jones scoring three tries. Tonight was Stacey Jones' night. He scored three tries . . . maybe one of them shouldn't have been allowed but two of them looked fine by me. To go out the way he did, and I pay homage to the crowd who stayed around. Tears were flowing, especially where I was standing, when Stacey Jones walked off the pitch. New Zealand has lost an icon but he's added to our folklore.'

Kemp had plenty of history behind him in becoming an ardent admirer of Jones, having ended his Kiwi career just as Jones was starting his and then sharing five years with him at the Warriors. Price had no such background but was no less effusive in his adulation. 'One of the things that excited me coming to the Warriors was to get to play with him,' he said. 'I tried to chase him around for 10 years and didn't catch him. Then I finally got the chance to play with him and he's leaving. He still hasn't set me up for a try yet. I've been close a couple of times. I don't know whether it means he doesn't like me or what. I got to play with Terry Lamb and some wonderful blokes at the Bulldogs and Stacey Jones is right up there with Terry Lamb, who I regard as one of the greatest clubmen this game has ever seen. I've had the absolute pleasure of spending 12 months with a guy that I absolutely admired as an opponent — both at international and club level — and now I've had the chance to play with him. It was a pleasure and an honour and to be accepted by his family as well. They are beautiful people. It's been awesome. It is something I will have for the rest of my life, a great little mate over in New Zealand.'

Not too many New Zealanders could have put it better but Jones was as reluctant as ever having people make a fuss of him. More one-on-one interviews followed outside the media conference room, each dutifully completed and, on the way back across the field, Jones just as obligingly attended to those who had waited for autographs and photos. He said he'd do them when he came back and he did.

Inside the gym, team-mate Wairangi Koopu was waiting equally patiently with a Maori TV crew for a pre-arranged interview; one that would be the last of the night finished with a lovely moment when the two men hugged each other.

Upstairs at the after-match function the crowd awaited Jones and gave him an ovation as he was predictably named the players' player of the day and winner of the game ball. More autographs to sign, more posing for photos, something to eat and a beer to drink — and then, at last, he could make his way to his big party at the Supertop on the other side of the ground and one last chance to say goodbye to the fans.

The night became morning but now it was definitely over, a year later than originally planned perhaps but there was no question the timing was far better than it would have been in 2004 . . .

Richard Becht
Auckland, September 2005

False alarm — just!

I'd seen it all at the Warriors. Coaches sacked or walking before they were shown the door, chief executives coming and going, players doing the same and all sorts of other drama, not least the club barely surviving after being brought to its financial knees a couple of times. But despite the trials, only once had I thought about moving on to another club that might have appealed as being a little more solid.

That was late in 2000 after the Warriors crumbled for the second time in two years. Even then, my preference was to stay if it was at all possible and, when Eric Watson came along to save the club, I was soon pleased to be able to say I was still a Warrior. I couldn't really imagine rugby league life any other way at that stage.

You never can be too sure what might crop up, though, and in my case a bad hand of cards began to fall in 2004. It was so bad I thought I had just two clear choices — and one of them wasn't staying at Ericsson Stadium.

The way I saw it, I could simply retire — even though I wasn't quite 28 — or I could leave Auckland behind to finish my playing days in the English Super League. I eventually eliminated the first option and settled on the second one, looking at a plan that would see me not just starting my top-level career as a Warrior but finishing as one as well — only with two different clubs.

It's incredible to recall this now but we were only a few weeks into the 2004 National Rugby League season when everything began to unravel for me, and for my favourite club, too, for that matter. I barely had time to catch my breath and there I was committed to leaving the club that had meant so much to me — the New Zealand Warriors — to start afresh with the Wigan Warriors. Since leaving school, the Warriors had dominated my entire adult life. I'd grown up with the place, marrying Rachelle, having our two daughters Chellcey and Waiana and setting ourselves up. I was a Warrior through and through but I was so ready to walk away. I can't quite describe how close it was to happening but let's just say that if certain orders had been followed to the letter there would have been no way back. Only some late manoeuvring prevented it coming to that, which didn't please some people, especially Wigan boss Maurice Lindsay and former Kiwi turned player manager Peter Brown who had put the deal together.

I suppose it was a fairly important detail but all they were missing was my signature on the contract I'd verbally agreed to — and I can tell you only some unusual circumstances stopped me signing. That's the way it goes in professional sport sometimes and, while Maurice and Pete will have other thoughts, I can only say I was glad things worked out differently in the end. That's because I know now it wouldn't have been the right way to end my time with the Vodafone Warriors, leaving on such a low after what became such a disappointing 2004 season. I've thought about it a lot since and I just couldn't have lived with it ending that way.

For a few weeks, though, I was absolutely convinced quitting the Warriors was the only logical option for me, provided the club was prepared to let me do so despite being contracted until the end of the 2006 season.

A lot of things rushed through my mind. I'd been committed to the club. I'd been involved from the outset, going way back to that fantastic first night on 10 March 1995. I wasn't with the first-grade side then but I was on the field in the curtain-raiser to the historic Winfield Cup match, running around with No 20 on my back for the reserve-grade side as we dished it out to the Broncos 36–14. Soon after I was as awestruck as any of the other 31,000-plus people in the crowd when Dean Bell led the Warriors out of the tunnel, through two rows of flames, past the Maori welcoming party and onto Ericsson Stadium.

Just a few weeks later, I couldn't believe I was playing alongside Dean and the rest of the guys, achieving my first-grade dream well ahead of my own schedule. And it all rolled on from there as I went on to experience so many club and personal milestones along the way. I loved the place and the people involved in it. I loved being able to live at home and follow my goal of becoming a rugby league professional. Of course, there were some uncertain times but I survived them and headed into the 2004 season knowing I was set to bring up my 200th appearance for the club.

Of my first nine seasons as a Warrior, the best times had come in the previous three years when, under Eric Watson's ownership, we finally delivered on the promise we'd shown from the outset. Three times we made the finals, we won the minor premiership and reached the grand final for the first time and came close to a repeat grand final a year later in 2003. And one of the most important ingredients in our success had been a previously unknown coach, Daniel Anderson. During those times he had so much to offer to all of us. Life was good, or so I thought until the plot started to change in 2004.

To explain why it came to that point, I need to go back a bit, probably to the end of the 2003 season. As I say, we'd just missed out on making back-to-back grand final appearances, beaten 28–20 by the Penrith Panthers who went on to win the title against the Roosters. To be honest, I wasn't really in any physical shape to be playing at all then. I was in constant pain from a groin injury which had been bothering me since the Anzac Test earlier in the year. I had to have some time out and I missed our next five games after that test as I tried to recover.

Understandably, Daniel wanted me to have a run before the play-offs, so in the last round of the regular season I started against Wests Tigers. I was feeling fine, too, until I slipped and the groin felt even worse than it had before. I left the field and from then on I basically couldn't train and needed to have four or five injections to get me through each game. The only run I'd have with the team would be the day before each match to make sure I knew the calls. Running was a problem and so was kicking, but I managed to struggle through as we beat the Bulldogs and then Canberra to leave us one win away from the grand final.

Exciting as it was for the players, the club and the fans, I actually couldn't wait for those games to finish. I was in agony and when we lost to Penrith — which was sad for everyone involved — my body was telling me it was glad the season was over. I honestly don't think I could have played in the grand final if we'd beaten the Panthers. That's how bad it was and that's why I had to pull out of the end-of-season test against the Kangaroos a few weeks later, being forced to watch instead as Ruben Wiki and the boys put together an awesome effort to win at North Harbour Stadium.

I was a crock then. The injury was giving me grief and I knew I'd probably need surgery to fix things up. With groin injuries, though, an operation is a last resort so a rehab approach was favoured by the medical staff. I'd had the injury before. That was in 1994 ahead of the club's first year in the Winfield Cup, yet even then it didn't improve until six months later. When I did it again during the 48–6 flogging the Aussies gave us in the 2003 Anzac Test in July, I immediately knew in my heart of hearts that I would need surgery. I'm not a medical expert but I just had that belief. You have to listen to your medical specialists, though; they were hoping things would work out through rehab and strengthening it up. After three months there was no real sign of improvement so, close to Christmas, a call had to be made — if I was to be ready for the start of the 2004 NRL season, I'd have to have an operation then, and I did. The damage was on my left side, and what they do to repair the problem is to cut the tendon away and it sort of grows back. Once I'd been operated on, I faced a recovery period of around 12 weeks before I'd be able to really rip back into full training. There was even some hope I'd be able to play in one or two trial matches but the groin just wasn't right. The reason it took so long to recover properly was because of the wear and tear from playing with the injury and the injections I'd had as well.

The end result was I was badly under-prepared as we set ourselves for our opening match against Brisbane. While there was no chance of me missing the game, I knew I wasn't right as we lost the match 28–20. That one didn't seem to worry Daniel that much. He brushed it aside — but when we lost at home to St George Illawarra (16–10) and Penrith (42–22) in the next two matches he started putting the heat on me. He told me I wasn't playing as I should have been, which was fair enough because I knew I wasn't. There were contributing factors, though, which he didn't seem prepared to acknowledge. Because I'd had such a limited build-up, I wasn't anywhere near prepared.

We had an off-season training programme that year where we didn't do a lot of aerobic work in any case, but I just wasn't ready and that was all there was to it. I know Daniel told the media I was right to go and that was the message we had to get across; it wasn't the real truth, though. While I was way better than I'd been at the end of the 2003 season, I hadn't been able to start full running until maybe a week before the season started. Anyone could see I was a long way behind the others.

Our fitness levels across the board weren't great, it had to be said. It was Daniel's idea that our off-season programme should be focused on power rather than the accepted method of mixing things up by building a strong aerobic base. It was a lot different from where we were at the end of 2003 when our fitness was the big thing that had enabled us to get through so many matches in the run-up to the finals and then in the following wins against the Bulldogs and the Raiders.

Put all of those factors together and the start to the 2004 season didn't play out the way we had hoped — we had a few losses, I wasn't playing up to the level I wanted because I wasn't adequately prepared and then suddenly confidence began to suffer across the team. Daniel had meetings with me after those opening three losses and asked me what was happening, but it was hard to say much when my confidence was down.

While we managed to stop the run of losses by beating Manly 28–10 in our fourth match of the year, we were back in trouble after losing at home to Newcastle. As well as our poor performances, there were other things going on that were making me feel unsettled. Rachelle remembers those times well, although not with any satisfaction.

The way she tells it, I was coming home with concerns about my future in the game because the club had started asking me about my plans to retire. I certainly remember rumours floating around at that time that I might quit. It reached the point where I rang my manager Peter Brown and he said he'd been meaning to ring me because he'd heard the Warriors were apparently looking for a second-rower and there'd also been word around that they could be looking to move me on at the end of the year. This was all coming out before the Ali Lauitiiti business flared up in public with his sudden departure. I guess it got me thinking a bit. With the way things were going for the team that season, the way I was playing and all these things being said, I began to wonder whether management was maybe trying to push me out. I don't know. All I know is that a lot of things go through your mind when your confidence is down, when pressure is going on the team from all directions and you're also getting it from the coach, as I was from Daniel.

I thought I was playing better than I had been in the first two or three games but crisis point was reached for our so-called away encounter with the Bulldogs in Wellington. After giving up a 12–0 halftime lead, I scored early in the second half to bring us back into it only for the Dogs to then grab two more tries and lead 24–6. We came back again to 24–12 to have the sniff of something but straight after that try the coach hooked me from the field with about 11 minutes to go. If nothing else, it made for an interesting interchange bench because also sitting there with me were Clinton Toopi and Ali Lauitiiti. While I was the captain and almost always played the full 80 minutes, I wasn't about to question Daniel's motives; he was the coach and he had to trust his instincts. Still, I'd be lying if I didn't say I was surprised to see the game out from the bench, watching the boys put in a late charge before being beaten 24–18.

There was another important issue going on at the same time that night. The match doubled as something of a trial for the Kiwi selectors with a number of contenders on show. The Bulldogs, led by soon-to-become-a-Warrior Steve Price, had New Zealand test hopefuls in Jamaal Lolesi, Matt Utai, Sonny Bill Williams and Roy Asotasi while we had any number of players hoping to make the cut despite our start to the year hardly helping selection claims.

Up in the media room, eyes were on the test contenders, but they didn't miss what happened to me either. While I didn't attend the media conference straight after the match — I wasn't in any sort of mood for it — I heard about it, and the line of questioning and the answers were revealing. Everyone worked out that something odd was going on and Daniel's replies to some of the questions only heightened suspicion. In part, the conference ran like this:

Stacey Jones — was there something wrong with him?
[Anderson:] No.

What has the match done in terms of Kiwi test team calculations?
Not much. We [the Warriors] had plenty of good players out there and from what I could see [of the Bulldogs] all their Kiwi boys were putting a dent in us. For the Kiwi selectors I think there were probably plenty of positives out there.

Is there any doubt about Stacey Jones being the [Kiwi] halfback?
It's not for me to comment on right here and now.
When you replaced him, what was behind that?
I thought we had to try to have a go at something. That was basically the reason.

Even if I had wanted to be at that conference I can't imagine I would have been welcome, not when you read those comments. And later back at our hotel I discovered just what was cooking when Daniel had a talk to me about the match and about the Kiwis. Tony Kemp was there, too, and Ando started to have a go at me. He told me he'd taken me off because I'd made a couple of mistakes that I shouldn't have made. I said that was fair enough. It didn't end there, though, because he then said I was gutless, that I wasn't showing what I was capable of and that if I didn't pull my finger out he'd drop me back to the domestic Bartercard Cup competition for our next match — but he'd still be picking me for the Anzac Test against the Aussies.

I didn't say too much but naturally I was pissed off at being called gutless. I told him: 'Bugger this. I'm going to stay home with the family next weekend then. I'm not going to play for you if you're going to talk to me like that.' After what I'd gone through in 2003 playing through with a serious injury I wasn't expecting that kind of treatment. Gutless? I don't think so. Maybe it was a case of a bit of sour grapes on my part but I was so angry this was happening. I guess it had all been building up to something because the season wasn't working out for us after losing five out of six games and you could see it was all starting to get to Daniel.

The match against the Bulldogs was played on a Friday night and the New Zealand team was due to be named on Sunday. I think by then Daniel had already picked his side and after that meeting Kempy, who was also Daniel's assistant coach with the Kiwis, rang me up and said: 'Come on Stace, we want you to play, mate.' I said my mind was made up. I wouldn't be available for the test, I'd be staying home and that was that. After all, if the coach said he was going to drop me back to Bartercard Cup, how then was I good enough to be playing for the Kiwis?

I went home and discussed my decision with Rachelle and my family. Their reaction was that it was a big call to make but at least they understood exactly how I was feeling about it. Of course it was a huge deal to say I wouldn't play for my country and I realised there would be an outcry from some quarters. It wasn't at all easy reaching that point, but the way it added up to me nothing at all would have changed my mind — and it didn't. If there'd been another Kiwi coach and I was going into a new environment it would have been different. When things weren't going so well at the Warriors from time to time it was always refreshing to go into camp with the Kiwis where the atmosphere changed from what I knew at the club. Then again, it was hypothetical in this case. The fact was the coach I had with the Warriors was also the Kiwi coach and he'd been dishing it out to me.

By Saturday, Daniel was on the phone saying he appreciated what my decision was, that he was comfortable with it and let's just get on with things. So on Sunday the test side came out without my name in it. I'd missed the 2003 end-of-season win over the Aussies and now I was out of this one as well. I didn't know it then but the truth was my test career was probably over. It seemed to have finished that night in Sydney when I'd injured my groin.

In fact, my entire career could have finished there and then. With what had gone on so far in the 2004 season and then the meeting in Wellington, I just couldn't see much point in playing on at that stage, not for the Warriors or for any other side. I talked with Rachelle about it and told her I simply wanted to end it all there, give it away and retire from football completely. It might sound unbelievable now but that's how much everything was eating away at me. There was a lot of time to think about things, too, because after the Bulldogs match we had the bye while Daniel headed off to prepare the Kiwis for the test in Newcastle. Those of us not involved in the test basically had the week off, so I was stewing and had time to consider things.

At exactly the same time, the Ali Lauitiiti situation blew up. He'd been left out of the test side as well and soon enough it was revealed he was leaving the club. That blew everyone away but basically it seemed to me that Ali just didn't have the appetite for NRL football any longer. He'd lost his desire and certainly we hadn't seen the best of him since he injured his knee before the finals in 2002 and then needed to have surgery to remove a cyst from his arm in 2003. Pete

Brown and mainly Frank Endacott were involved in finding Ali a deal at Leeds and I had also been talking to Pete about my situation. He told me he could set me up with a club in England and it seemed like the only option that was worth pursuing for me, if I was to keep playing at all.

When Ando came back from the test I told him this was going to be my last season with the Warriors. Either I would move on to play in England or I would retire from football entirely. Signing for another NRL club wasn't a consideration at all. I was in my 10th season with the Warriors and believed I'd had a fair crack at it. It wasn't going to be so straightforward. I knew that.

My thoughts about retiring were genuine so, as a way of keeping me in Auckland, Ando and CEO Mick Watson put an idea to me to take up an assistant coach's job in 2005. It wasn't going to be so much an assistant coaching job as a role where I looked after the junior players in a mentoring sort of position and maybe helped players in the NRL squad with kicking skills. While it was nice to be thought of like that I couldn't see it working at all.

What was important was that everyone now agreed I wasn't going to be with the Warriors after the 2004 season. With that in mind, Ando told me he was going to shift me from halfback to standoff for the rest of the year. Once a bloke says he wants to leave the club then it makes total sense to look at alternatives for the future so the move was sweet by me. There were also signs of regret from Daniel about the way he'd handled my predicament. He admitted it had been a bad move telling me I would be dropped to the Bartercard Cup if I didn't measure up. He said he knew he shouldn't have said that.

As the days went by, I eliminated retirement from my plans and warmed towards the idea of playing in England. When I asked Mick whether I could have permission to sign with an English club he gave it the all-clear, saying there was no way he could keep a player at the club if he didn't want to be there. As it happened, Pete and Frank were heading to England to catch up with some of their players —

including Ali at Leeds — so Pete also focused on lining up a deal for me, Wigan and Hull FC being the two options he was looking at. None of this stopped me fronting up and putting in for the Warriors, although the environment wasn't that great at all with Ando. In our matches against Melbourne, North Queensland — my 200th first-grade appearance — Manly, South Sydney and the Roosters, I ran in the No 6 jersey. We were still in a battle zone trying to figure out how to win matches and it was clear to me that our off-season training programme — and our lack of aerobic fitness — was working against us. There was friction, too, between Ando and Kempy. They weren't talking to each other and hadn't been since the start of the season. They were in their fourth year as a coaching combination and had always seemed to operate well in the past but now there was a wall between them. As he had always done, Kempy talked to me a lot, though.

When I first came into the Kiwis in 1995, he was just finishing his test career and we'd been working together at the Warriors all that time so we had a good relationship. For all that, training sessions had become very strange — Ando would be at one end of the field and Kempy would be at the other end. They wouldn't acknowledge each other; it was just bizarre after everything they'd been through together.

Against that backdrop, the drums were beginning to beat about my future in England. The day we clashed with the Roosters in Sydney — 30 May — the *Sunday Star-Times* ran with this story:

English Super League clubs will be lining up to talk about Stacey Jones' rugby league future when player managers Peter Brown and Frank Endacott head to England late next week.

The 28-year-old's been the subject of intense speculation and, while no one will confirm it, all indications are he'll finish with the New Zealand Warriors at the end of this NRL season despite having another two seasons to run on his contract.

It's expected Jones will soon make a decision on his next move with retirement thought to be one of his options.

If he continues to play, then it's believed his future would lie with an English club.

After missing out on Warriors reject Ali Lauitiiti, Wigan would be the logical favourite to sign the champion halfback, now playing at standoff for the Warriors. They'll be cashed up and need a halfback with former Roosters No 7 Adrian Lam quitting.

Reports this week also have Hull FC coach Shaun McRae expressing an interest in any race for Jones' signature. McRae has been associated with the Kiwis in an assistant coach's capacity in the past.

Jones has previously dismissed the talk as being 'silly rumours', adding: 'I still want to help this club to win a premiership. It's a goal of mine. I'm looking to go through to the end of 2006 and who knows, there might be another year after that.'

It's significant, though, that Lance Hohaia has been given the scrumhalf's job and the key playmaking role since returning from his knee surgery, so providing a contingency plan for life after Jones, should that come about.

With results running against him — just three wins in the first 10 matches — rumours began to build that Ando might not stick around too much longer and that we'd soon have a new coach. Kempy told me that if he was given the job he wanted me to stay and he wanted me to play halfback; if he missed out and left to go elsewhere, he said he wanted me to come with him.

It wasn't long before the rumour became fact. We were flogged 58–6 by the Roosters in a dreadful performance. It was totally embarrassing but Ando started the new week like any other. When he named his side on Tuesday for our next match against Canberra I was again selected at standoff but by Thursday Ando had gone, quitting after we'd won only three of our first 11 matches.

It was a weird day. Word had got out overnight that something big had happened at a meeting between Mick and Ando late on the Wednesday. Eric was in town and when we all arrived at the club as usual we found television news cameras, photographers and journalists all around the place. It's fair to say there was quite a bit of chat going on among the players — and there was no sign of Ando. That morning we were told he'd finished up and that Kempy now had the job, at least on a temporary basis.

I can't say I was too sad about the outcome, not after what had gone on since the start of the year. However, I'll also be the first to say Daniel did a terrific job in his first three seasons when he'd proved he was a very good coach. He'd certainly helped a lot of us with our games, but in the end there were just too many issues with him.

As soon as Kempy was given control he immediately told me I'd be back at halfback against the Raiders. It was a Sunday afternoon match so there wasn't a lot of time to fine-tune our preparation and, of course, there was massive media coverage about Daniel's exit and about the state the club was in just weeks after Ali had also left. We couldn't afford to be too sidetracked by it.

When game day arrived, it was emotional for all sorts of reasons, not least because Ando had walked out and Kempy was having his first match in full charge. We had to get back on track somehow. The decision was made not just to play me at halfback but also to switch jersey numbers, so I ran out in my favoured No 7. It was against the NRL's rules to do that but Mick believed risking a fine was worth it in the circumstances.

I've been involved in some dramatic days but this was surely one of the most extraordinary. There was just so much passion running through the side, arguably too much as we got up and gave it to the Raiders with a 20–14 win. When I say too much, that was proven by the aftermath when the judiciary hammered us with three players — Jerry Seuseu, Francis Meli and Sione Faumuina — being suspended for a total of 16 matches. We won, though, and at the time that was vital, even though it turned out to be a false dawn.

None of this — Ando going and Kempy taking over — had changed my mind about anything. I was set on going and was working towards that outcome. It wasn't just the Daniel business, although that was a very big part of it. The year had made me realise that I'd been on the NRL scene long enough and that I needed to pack up and move on. Being in the one place for so long had gradually worn me down I think. I'd been happy with my lot until then, more than happy. I loved being able to have a professional career while living in my hometown. That suited me perfectly and I'd never been interested in looking elsewhere.

Now my future was taking shape. Pete had stitched together a deal with Wigan that offered some very good money, although that wasn't a big reason for wanting to move. I'd always been comfortable with my deal at the Warriors and would have been happy with it if I'd stayed. There was a bigger picture now.

Mick and I talked regularly about my plans and everything was right on track, especially when Pete arrived home with a contract for me to sign. I'd been having meetings or discussions with Pete and Frank throughout and nothing, it seemed, was going to stop me seeing it through, although there was some pressure building in the media for the club to stand firm, as this story published in the *Sunday Star-Times* on 20 June indicated:

An impasse is brewing between the New Zealand Warriors and Stacey Jones' player management team over the champion halfback's rugby league future.

It's believed manager Peter Brown, along with his business partner Frank Endacott, met Jones on Friday night to discuss firm offers they'd brought home with them from a two-week trip to England.

Brown and Endacott were in England ostensibly to connect with players on their books, including Wigan's former Kiwi prop Quentin Pongia and Bradford's ex-Kiwi back row forward Logan Swann, but it's known Jones' plans were also discussed.

While he's contracted to the end of 2006 a range of issues, including Jones' apparent differences with now-departed Warriors coach Daniel Anderson, prompted English Super League clubs to show an interest in signing the apparently disaffected player. Since Ali Lauitiiti's exit from the Warriors, Jones' name has regularly been linked with the likes of Wigan, Hull FC and St Helens, although the player himself insisted as recently as a week ago that he wasn't thinking beyond this season.

There has also been constant innuendo about Jones seeking a release from his contract; chief executive Mick Watson recently said it would be possible if it was the only course of action open to both parties.

But since Tony Kemp replaced Anderson as coach, the Warriors' resolve has hardened. They don't seem to be in the mood to release their best player when they agreed to sign him on such a long-term basis.

Kemp, who's highly likely to become the Warriors' coach on a permanent basis next year, said: 'I don't want Stacey to go. I hold him in high regard and he knows that.'

Said Jones last week: 'I think some people might think I'm being shoved out the door here but that's not it at all. The club's been good and Kempy's being supportive.'

Just two weeks ago against Canberra, Kemp switched the 28-year-old straight back to scrumhalf after Anderson's experiment using him at standoff. Jones responded with his best performance of the year but was unable to express himself in last Sunday's dismal loss to Wests Tigers.

With the NRL's anti-tampering deadline coming off on June 30, Jones' contract situation is critical as the club prepares to hit the player market, but it's clear Watson is headed for a testing if not testy showdown with Brown and Endacott in the next few days. Progress in any talks will have a significant bearing on other players' contracts as well.

That was fairly close to the money because only a day or two later everything changed. What happened was that one process wasn't completed. Frank had told Pete to see Mick to get a written release for me down on paper. That wasn't done, though. There was no signed release so I couldn't sign the contract and that ultimately proved to be the key that kept me in New Zealand. We wouldn't be talking about this now if that detail had been attended to.

There was another big factor — Eric Watson. He was still home from England and now he became involved. I went out to his place at Karaka with a few of the players to have some drinks one day and Eric said: 'I want you to stay.' Mick was there as well and he said the club wanted me to carry on for one more year and then see how I felt.

I didn't know what to say because I had agreed with Pete that I would go to Wigan. Eric and Mick kept talking to me, saying it wouldn't be a good note to leave on and that they were going to go hard-out for some big signings. Mick showed me a list of players he was looking to chase and asked me which players I'd be keen on and I said: 'If I was in the team, I'd want Pricey (Steve Price) and Rubes (Ruben Wiki) straight away.' It didn't mean I was saying I would stay if those players were signed, it was really just a matter of him showing me what he was trying to do, but the parting request that day was: 'Stace, stay for one more year.'

They'd won me over. I went home, talked about it with Rachelle and rang Pete to say I wouldn't be going to Wigan after all. Knowing how much work he and Frank had done putting the deal together, I felt quite bad but in the end I'd been turned around and appreciated the value of being able to stay one more year. If I'd gone it would have been a bad way to finish with the club.

Having made the call to stay, I wasn't so sure about what followed, though. It was decided there should be a media conference at Ericsson Stadium to announce I would be staying, to end all the speculation there had been. I was there with Mick in front of the cameras and journalists, answering questions and doing interviews. I was uncomfortable with that. I thought there should have just been a basic announcement made through a media release but nothing more than that.

Everything had come to a head in the days after our heart-breaking 28–26 loss to North Queensland. The club wanted to generate some positive news in a tough year and I suppose this was one way of doing it, although we then slumped to another heavy defeat a few days later against Melbourne. It was one long season that just wasn't going to finish soon enough for a lot of us.

While I wasn't that crazy about having a media conference, it did at least provide a chance to put a message out there for the public because there had been a lot of talk about what was going on. Knowing what we all do now, it's worth looking closely at what Mick said at the conference: 'The reason we got together was not so much to make an announcement but to make a statement that Stacey Jones will be staying with the club and continuing his journey of being a one-club man at the Warriors and he'll hopefully finish his playing career with the Warriors in the NRL. I think it's crucial for New Zealand. When you've got your heroes, you don't want them to finish abroad. I think it would be a beautiful thing if Stacey Jones finished his career where he started. That would be a perfect finish.'

The key words there were 'he'll hopefully finish his playing career with the Warriors in the NRL'. For weeks I'd struggled with media interviews, knowing things were happening but not being able to give the full story. At least I could explain myself and it's interesting now to stay in the moment and look back at the answers I gave to some questions that day:

Did you have a choice to go elsewhere?
There were options there. The club wouldn't have stood in my way if I had wanted to move on but I feel I want to stick with the Warriors. It's been a struggle this year and I feel it's not a good way to go out. Looking at the future of the club, I can see things happening for us. I've been through bad times but I can see good times coming.

How did Daniel Anderson's departure affect your decision?
Not at all . . . if Daniel was still the coach it would have been the same. I really enjoyed playing under Daniel but we've moved on now to Tony Kemp.

What swayed you to stay?
I've been here so long and you don't want to leave on a disappointing note. The club has some good things put in place for the future. I feel like I have a lot to offer this club. My oldest daughter has just started school and she's loving it, and your family is important. The things we have in New Zealand . . . we're very lucky. The things I like to do outside of football I really enjoy and I wouldn't get those sorts of opportunities elsewhere. First and foremost it was

a family decision. Obviously there was a fair amount of speculation and the players were asking me. I was being honest with the players I'm close with but it wasn't that hard to make the decision.

Did you talk to Eric [Watson] about your plans?
We spoke about it. He was away most of the time the club and I had been talking so he wasn't really in the picture. Since he has been back he has told me he really wants me to stay and to get that sort of reassurance is pretty good. He said if I went to England we would catch up but if I stayed it would be great. He was really supportive.

Is there an opening to revisit this in one year or is it a case of you seeing it right through now?
That's the commitment but Mick has said, see how you go next year and it's open to you. But I feel if I'm going to stay I might as well stay for the long haul. It's something the club is open to but, at my age, is it worth going to England at the end of next year with just a year left?

Was this fairly much you and Rachelle talking this through or was it a wider family decision?
It was just us. It was up to me. Rachelle was supportive. She had her opinion but she said it was up to me. She would go to England but she wanted me to do what I thought was best.

I can say now that what I thought was best was certainly the right choice because, ahead of me, there would be an 11th and last season with the Warriors that made me so glad I stayed. Not that the end of my 10th season was anything like I wanted it to be, though. We really battled through the final weeks with some ugly defeats along the way.

I've been on the end of some bad days with the club but the 50–4 loss to Wests Tigers in Christchurch was down there with the worst of them, and there was nothing too special either about defeats that followed when we played Melbourne, Parramatta and the Bulldogs.

By then, though, there was something to look forward to — the end of a season that couldn't come soon enough and the thought of an off-season that offered so much in the way of hope and excitement. That had been provided by the club making a big splash on the player market. First, experienced Cowboys halfback Nathan Fien was signed; that was a smart move, probably done when it looked like I was definitely leaving. Then two huge announcements followed within days of each other in July — one week Kiwi captain Ruben Wiki was confirmed as a Warrior, at last coming home after 12 seasons with Canberra, and the next week Bulldogs skipper Steve Price's signing was announced. Just a few weeks earlier, when Eric and Mick asked me to stay, I'd told them Rubes and Pricey were the two players on their shopping list that would be fantastic signings. I never really thought it would happen but now we had both of them. Then, after our season had finished, we discovered Roosters winger Todd Byrne was also on his way to Auckland.

That perked me up about 2005 in a big way and it still wasn't finished with two of my great former team-mates, Ivan Cleary and Kevin Campion, also heading back 'home' to join the coaching team. With Kempy confirmed as head coach, Ivan and Campo on board, Tony Iro part of the mix as well plus the new players coming, everything was looking good.

Ahead of me lay a year I'd treasure. I was made a life member of the club before the 2005 NRL season started. That blew me away. If that wasn't enough, there was talk about having a testimonial as well. At first there was an idea there could have been a match of some sort using some of the blokes I'd played with and against during my career but that was always going to be far too difficult to achieve. So that became a testimonial luncheon instead, organised by the Mad Butcher. That was an unbelievable occasion and so, too, was my last appearance at Ericsson Stadium against Newcastle — and against Andrew Johns. Lion Red even produced beer in my name, which floored me as well.

Looking at it all that way, I know the choice to stay was the right one. That was all to come, though. What I did know was that I wouldn't be finishing my career as I started it, as a Warrior either in Auckland or in England. What I didn't know was just where the final destination would be but, as I discovered, I was about to be presented with an exotic opportunity I couldn't resist.

Je m'appelle Stacey Jones

I'd made the decision to stay. That wasn't a problem. That's how I wanted it to be but whether I saw through the last two years of the contract was another story. I had the attitude that I might as well finish it off properly, or at least that's what I said, but I also saw some merit in making 2005 my last year at Ericsson Stadium.

For one, I could obviously see we had a much-improved squad; it was one we all believed would put the club back on the right path. With the big buys, Steve Price and Ruben Wiki, we inherited enormous experience and ability, two of the best forwards in the whole competition. And with former North Queensland halfback Nathan Fien and ex-Roosters winger Todd Byrne joining us as well, we had two more capable professionals.

Huge effort went into reshaping the club in every way, not just through tweaking the playing roster. There was also a completely different look to the coaching structure with Kempy heading it up and Ivan and Campo with him. Tony Iro had been signed on as the IT and video analyst and John Ackland was with us as the football development manager. It would take time to find out how all the pieces fitted together but I could see some real merit in it. As senior players, we'd been kept in the picture and we supported what was being done.

There was also a physical change in the sense that we moved addresses. The club's original home opposite the gates on the eastern side of Ericsson Stadium was about to become our former home. By Christmas we were able to move into a new base in the completed East Stand. That couldn't come soon enough. We'd been at the old base since the club started and it had become rundown and a bit stale as an environment. There were good memories there from the great times in 2001, 2002 and 2003 but there'd been plenty of bad ones, too, a decent share of them coming in 2004. What we had in store for us was a huge new gym, great facilities, new offices and all of this right inside Ericsson Stadium. It couldn't be any better than that. Being able to make a clean cut from the past to head into a new start in every way was a real plus.

Until that could happen, we took a clean break from the environment completely, shifting temporarily to the new Trusts Stadium in Waitakere City where we were based for the two months or so of our training programme pre-Christmas. Some of the boys were missing at first with Steve, Nathan and Todd not with us full-on until a few weeks into the off-season schedule, while Ruben and the others in the Kiwis were given a break after the Tri Nations series. But it was there, at Trusts Stadium, that we worked on changes in philosophy and attitude. We trained like we hadn't trained before, well, not for a long time anyway. In the space of a few weeks we were trying to make up for all the work we hadn't done in our preparation for the 2004 season. Kempy, Ivan and Campo rated fitness the priority and we were given a flogging. We needed it, too, but there was plenty of variety to keep it interesting, if you could call it that.

If we weren't labouring up the monster sand hills at Bethells Beach we were being worked in the sand and surf at Mairangi Bay by surf life-saving champion Cory Hutchings, taking on One Tree Hill, running around the Auckland Domain, hitting the weights in our makeshift gym and also being put through some tough wrestling training. There was also some track work, conditioning sessions on the field and ball work and we really felt it, some more than others. Nathan collapsed one day and there were some great pictures of Ruben staggering around during a brutal conditioning session when he first joined us. He didn't look too flash and he had to excuse himself from a string of media interviews he was meant to do that day, but the message he sent out to all of us was a strong one. While he was struggling, he kept going. He finished the session and survived it and that's the way it needed to be all year. Keep going, don't stop.

The toughest part of the lot, though, came when we had a few days at the Waiouru Army Camp. It was meant to be a surprise destination, or a shock one, when we were loaded onto a bus and taken to the railway station. Most of us had figured out what was happening by then but, if the surprise had been removed, we were still in for a shock because those days in Waiouru were just hell. By then we were in great physical condition — our skin-fold tests were amazing — and that camp was designed to work not just on physical endurance but on our mental toughness under duress.

It was during the gruelling off-season and pre-season training programme that I started to form clear thoughts about what I wanted to do. I was feeling fitter than I had for a long time. It was a good feeling, too. The team was coming together well and I was confident we were in for a decent season. So I thought, what better way than to finish up at the end of 2005? The way I saw it, I wanted to put everything into the training programme and then make the season as good as I possibly could before ending my time with the Warriors.

There was something else in the mix, though, that was appealing about moving on. Physically I was in decent shape but I knew one more year in the NRL would be close to enough for me. When you play 11 years in a competition of this standard, it has to have an effect on you and I know it was having a bit of an impact on me and on what I could do. I could have kept going and finished up at the Warriors but I felt a fresh environment at this late stage of my career was exactly what I needed — and I could also go on my terms. But back to that something else . . .

It cropped up as we were full throttle into our campaign at our Waitakere City base — and this wasn't an attraction just for me but for a number of us at the club. It turned out that Cullen Sports had been looking into the possibility of buying the financially troubled London Broncos franchise in the English Super League. And that opened up a chance not just for me but for a lot of other people tied up with the Warriors.

The name the Broncos usually means one thing to most people with a general sporting interest — Brisbane. That also means success on and off the field. No one could say that about the London version. Efforts to make rugby league a going concern in England's capital city had met with one failure after another. Nothing, it seemed, could make it work, but now Cullen Sports — and Mick was involved in this — had a view that it might be worth a closer look. While they were aware of all the traps, it still didn't make it a total non-starter. Rachelle and I were excited about it. We weren't the only ones. Mick was talking about quite a few of us going to London if the deal came off — Awen, Monty, Ivan and Campo as well. There was a thought then that we could have sister clubs — the Warriors in the NRL and the London Broncos in the English Super League. There'd be a chance for young New Zealand players to play with us in London and learn more about the game before going home to play NRL football. It could have been a good way to develop our players and get them ready before putting them into the NRL with the Warriors. So obviously the idea of having one last year at home and then heading to London was fine by me. I liked it.

That was the dream, and maybe that's all it ever was because it didn't turn out to be much more than that in the end, despite the speculation. As I understand it, the numbers just never stacked up. The Broncos had a history of serious financial troubles and it just wasn't worth Cullen Sports considering the venture so that one went away, back on the shelf and not to be considered again. We put it out of our minds, too, and all got on with the business of preparing for the 2005 NRL season.

Throughout the summer months, I talked to Mick a lot about the way things were going with the team and about how I was finding it all. Then, not long before the season started, we confirmed 2005 would be my last season with the Warriors, not that we told everyone about it. It was just an understanding we'd had all along. Mick was great about it and appreciated that I really wanted to finish in the NRL and go onto something new, as much for a lifestyle change as anything. It was nothing to do with the set-up at the Warriors. I couldn't have been happier with it after what had happened in 2004 but I sensed during the off-season that my time had definitely come in the NRL. I just couldn't see myself going through another off-season and one more year of playing in the toughest sporting competition I know.

I was free to make a move, to look around for a place for Rachelle and me to take the kids to finish off my playing days. About two weeks before the season started, Mick called me into his office and asked me whether I had any plans yet for 2006. I said I wasn't sure at that stage. I knew I could leave earlier if I wanted to but there hadn't been any approaches from other clubs and I hadn't been actively chasing one either. Then Mick turned around a whiteboard with some players' names on it. There was one list of players the club would have to let go and there was also a list of those who would be staying; I can confirm my name definitely wasn't among those who were to go.

I didn't think too much about it but about a week later I received a call from Paul Donkin. He'd been our football manager when Daniel Anderson was coach but left the club not long after Ando finished and now he was assistant coach with the French club Union Treiziste Catalane (UTC) in Perpignan, in the south of France. Also known as Les Catalans, they were looking to sign players as they put together a side for their first crack at the English Super League in 2006. Donks thought I was off contract and asked me what my plans were for the 2006 season. I told him I still had another year to go with the Warriors — which was true — but I got off the phone, told Rachelle what the call was about and straight away she said: 'Come on, let's go.' It was that simple. No other club had approached me. This one just landed in my lap at the perfect time. Bearing in mind the plan to go to London had fallen through, this was a chance we couldn't ignore. It just immediately felt like the best thing I could do as a player and we could do as a family.

Having told Mick I wasn't sure what my plans for 2006 were, I was soon back letting him know they had suddenly changed and that we now had a good reason to want to move on. Mick said he didn't have an issue, that he appreciated what I had done in 2004 when I agreed to stay for one more year and that he didn't believe there would be any London deal after all. I could stay if I wanted to but I was also assured of his support if I wanted to move elsewhere in 2006. I know a lot is said about players being released from contracts early. Some people seem to think it doesn't happen at any other club apart from the Warriors. That's certainly not true. Anyone who studies the player market every year would have noticed how many players become available despite having time to run on their contracts. I think every case has to be looked at on its merits. There are all sorts of reasons why players and clubs part company ahead of schedule, too many to go into right now. Sometimes the club is the driver, sometimes the player is. In my case, there was an understanding I could make a choice either way but Mick needed to know at an early stage so planning could begin for 2006.

At that meeting he offered to help with the contract, acting as my manager in effect to negotiate the deal with Donks and UTC. I had suggested I'd bring in Pete to work on the arrangement. After all, I'd had him around to handle my affairs before but Mick said he'd stitch up a deal for me for nothing and so we went about it that way. UTC offered something, Mick would counter and back and forth it went until the package was sorted out. I felt really comfortable with the arrangement working that way, even though Mick was filling two roles. It seemed kind of strange at first because I'd had Pete as my manager for my last contract with the Warriors but it worked out well this way as far as I was concerned. It was clean for me and for the two clubs involved.

I knew about UTC and the English Super League venture before this came about. I was also aware Donks was involved and that one of my former Warriors team-mates, Justin Murphy, was on the playing roster. As well as that I'd caught up with the fact that former Cronulla forwards Chris Beattie and Matt Bickerstaff were signed as was ex-Newcastle standoff Sean Rudder who had arrived after a stint with Castleford. That was about the extent of my knowledge, but I'd never given any thought to me being involved — until Donks made contact, that is.

I'd been to France before, to Perpignan no less, for a test there with the Kiwis in 2002. So when this came up, Rachelle and I were instantly hooked, getting the atlas out and having a decent look at where Perpignan was and studying all the places around it — and we were just blown away when we realised what was in store. No disrespect to the north of England, but the thought of living in the south of France had a lot going for it. To think we'd be able to live somewhere like that while playing in the English Super League . . . I didn't need any convincing. The idea of taking in the French way of life and the country's culture was too much to resist. As well as that, there was the attraction of being able to travel around Europe when time allowed. Spain is only half an hour away, the sea is right there — which means fishing for me — while Perpignan is at the foot of the Pyrenees. Soon after I'd made the decision, I saw John Kirwan at the Warriors one day and he told me he and his family weren't that far away in Italy, about 10–11 hours by car. He said we should come over when we got there — or he'd come across to see us. We were sold. Who wouldn't be? As long as the contract could be sorted out, there wouldn't be a doubt about it.

Donks was aware what I was earning at the Warriors so I told him if he could match it or come very close to it we'd have a deal, and he came straight back with the numbers that suited me. Once we'd reached that point I wanted all sorts of questions answered about the coaching staff, the playing roster, the cost of living and just about every little thing concerned with living in France. I wanted to know things like that. From what I could find out, the only items that are really expensive in France are petrol (then again, that was getting bloody expensive at home as well) and meat. It doesn't look like meat will be a problem anyway — not because the Mad Butcher is going to freight some to me but because the club owner there has an abattoir.

While the language is a bit hard, the experience of going to France is brilliant for young kids and we're not the least bit worried; it'll be fantastic for Chellcey and Waiana. Speaking and understanding French will be more of a challenge for Rachelle and me. That's why we started French lessons straight away. It was slow going at first, especially for me, but it's no surprise I made a point of finding out how to ask for a beer as quickly as possible, although I'm not so sure I'll be able to find the old Lion Rouge over there. Maybe Gordon Gibbons will have to see me right.

If I'd been worried only about a football contract I think it's fair to say I would have been looking at a club other than one in France. But at 29, with maybe two more years to go, this deal wasn't just about playing. What it provided in lifestyle and opportunities for us as a family was equally important and that's why UTC stacked up so well.

The quality of the club probably leaves a few unanswered questions but I accepted that. It's basically a start-up club, jumping out of the French competition which isn't so hot into the English Super League. That's what makes it even more exciting. It's a bit like going back to the days when the Warriors came into existence. We wanted to make it into the Winfield Cup, we were given the chance and then a whole lot of effort had to go into building the club and a team. I think that was a reason why UTC wanted me because I'd been through it at the Warriors and I've also found out over the years about issues like travel, which we'll have plenty of going to England every second week or so.

In this case the club exists but there's so much to be done to make Les Catalans competitive in the English competition. In that regard we've been given some help. We've been granted dispensation to have more imports than the clubs in England so, apart from me, Canberra back rowers Ian Hindmarsh and Michael Howell were signed along with Kiwi and Melbourne prop Alex Chan, Newcastle fullback Mark Hughes and utility forward, John Wilson, from Wests Tigers. That helped to beef the squad up a lot. Steve Deakin is the coach and David Waite's also involved, in the same sort of role John Hart has with the Warriors. He's there to be a mentor for the coaches and, with his experience coaching Newcastle, St George and Great Britain in the past, he has credentials for the job. As well as that Matt Adamson, who finished his playing career with Canberra this year, will be at Les Catalans as our trainer and Brad Fittler is also going to be involved helping promote the club, so there's a good list of people lined up.

I also see this as important for rugby league in a wider sense. The game needs to have some strength in France. Back in the 1950s the French were a real force internationally and even into the 1980s they were still very difficult to beat at home, especially before neutral referees came along. The Kiwis were beaten there in a test in 1980 and Australia lost both tests in 1978. So many people think rugby league doesn't have enough to offer at test level but, if UTC can make an impact, then there's a chance things could begin to improve. I'd like to think that's what will happen.

The owner, Bernard Guasch, and coach, Steve Deakin, came to Auckland around the time my signing was announced and, after meeting them, I felt a lot more relaxed about everything. Paul Donkin was also around when we were in Australia to play Newcastle on 17 April. He had a contract with him then and that's when things really began to take shape. It was a difficult time for me because I was trying to concentrate on doing my job for the Warriors and there was so much speculation around about what I was going to do. As usual some information was being leaked out from somewhere and I was getting irritated with what was being said in the media. There were claims I had signed for UTC already, which I hadn't done. I remember things were being said the weekend we were in Christchurch to play

Wests Tigers on 9 April. We'd just come off a decent win against South Sydney and were looking for our first case of back-to-back victories in a long time. Throughout the weekend, management was fielding inquiries about my future, looking for comment about rumours I was leaving. Because there was so much being said, we decided it would be best to put out this media release about the situation on 10 April:

Vodafone Warriors halfback Stacey Jones and CEO Mick Watson today responded to speculation about the veteran player's future with the NRL club.

After reading weekend media reports that he might be leaving the club at the end of the season, the 28-year-old Jones said his only focus right now was on the Vodafone Warriors.

'My total commitment is to our 2005 campaign,' he said after playing his 220th NRL match in his side's loss to Wests Tigers in Christchurch last night.

'I've just been made the club's first life member and have a huge respect for the Vodafone Warriors. I owe them so much.

'As one of the senior players I regularly chat to Mick about my role at the club and I've always had the chance to look at other options.

'What happens in the future is something I'll talk about with Mick when the time is right. I'm fully aware of the club's plans but right now it's all about winning football games for me.'

Watson echoed Jones' thoughts.

'Stacey Jones is playing good football this season and is driving this club on the field,' he said.

'Stacey and I will talk about his future nearer to June 30 [when the NRL's anti-tampering ban expires].

'We will decide what is right for the future and what is the best pathway for Stacey, his family and the club.

'Right now he and I alike are focused on just one thing — on-field performance and the Vodafone Warriors finishing in the play-offs.'

Anyone reading between the lines could have seen something was going on. A week later, there was more talk again and that's when I decided enough was enough. To me, the tone of what was being said suggested I had my mind on other things and that the Warriors weren't important to me. That's what hurt. I was completely committed to the club for the season, as I had planned to be from the moment we started our off-season programme. When the possibility of going to London fell over there was a danger I could have knocked off a bit, but that wasn't a consideration at all. As I say, it was annoying me that some people were having a dig at me so we put our heads together and put out another release, basically asking everyone to leave me alone and let me get on with playing football:

Vodafone Warriors halfback Stacey Jones says he's had a gutsful of continued speculation about his future.

'I just want to be left alone to play football,' he said from Newcastle yesterday as he built up to the Warriors' NRL encounter with the Knights later today.

'I'm sick of people going on about things that have nothing to do with them. It's my business and no one else's.'

Jones said he was frustrated and angry that his commitment to the Warriors was being questioned.

'I'm really enjoying my football at the club this year and I've been reasonably pleased with my own form,' he said.

'I've just been made a life member by the club. Everything about the Warriors means so much to me.

'I'm absolutely committed to doing all I can to make us a finals club again this year. That attitude won't change.

'I don't understand why people keep going on about things. I've had a gutsful of it — just leave me alone and let me get on with my job at the Warriors.'

While all of this was unfolding, our 2005 NRL season hadn't long been under way. We'd made an average beginning against Manly in our first match of the season before rebounding with a great win in Brisbane. I don't know what it is with us when we play the Broncos but we've found out what it takes to get over them. For the first half of the club's life, we couldn't get across the line at all, losing every time despite coming really close a couple of times. But from the time we beat them for the first time in 2001, we've basically had their measure and our 24–12 win at Suncorp Stadium was our sixth in nine matches against them.

After that we settled into a pattern we could have done without, our wins followed immediately by losses — the Cowboys beat us 32–22, we did South Sydney 46–14, went down to the Tigers 24–6 and then had an incredible result when we came back from 20–0 down to beat Newcastle 30–26. That was the first phase of our season as we looked towards a bye on the same weekend the Kiwis played Australia in the Anzac Test in Brisbane. Having retired from international football, I was again unavailable for that match and it was then that Mick and I tied things up with UTC and I signed a letter of intent. We'd hoped to have it sorted out by that stage so we could announce it the week of the bye. It made sense to do it then because we could get it out of the way without it affecting our preparation for a match. Some people apparently saw it differently. They thought we were driving this to come out to overshadow the test. That was stupid. We wanted to have it all cleared up so we'd be able to start the following week without any distractions as we looked ahead to our home fixture against Penrith on 1 May.

I guess there wasn't any real surprise when we made the announcement in the end on 21 April, the day before the test. There'd been a lot of speculation about it so the next step was to confirm it one way or the other. The fact is I couldn't have said anything any earlier. You can't comment about moving to a club until you've sealed the deal and that was possible only after I'd signed a letter of intent the day before the announcement was made. The signing of the final contract was still to come as we sorted through a few more details.

It's my nature that I didn't want to make a big fuss of it. In fact, if I'd had my way I would have preferred the club to simply put out a media release and leave it at that. I didn't see the need for a media conference or any interviews — just let me get on with playing for the Warriors. That's how I felt about it. Of course it wasn't going to be that easy. I could see the club's viewpoint that this needed to be handled differently. I'd been with the Warriors from the outset so I had to accept there would be a media conference for an announcement of this importance. We talked about the way it could be done. I was nervous about it. I'm not big on being in the spotlight at times like this. I don't think anyone is really, but especially not me. I realised I would have to say something so I agreed I'd make some comments at the conference after the announcement had been made. I wasn't at all interested in taking questions or doing interviews. I didn't see the need and didn't want to do that — but, boy, did that backfire on me. I came up with some thoughts which I had put down on paper. I figured having some comments written down and then reading them out was the best way to go about it. It was strange really. I was excited to know I'd sorted out what I would be doing, but I was on edge that this was being made into such a big deal because the media seemed to want it that way. I didn't see the need at all.

It's just as well we didn't have a game that week because there was a lot of pressure building up about the announcement. I can recall it all clearly now. The conference was staged in the Cullen Sports suite in the West Stand at Ericsson Stadium. When we walked in, there were plenty of cameras and reporters crammed into the room. A couple of the guys were there giving me moral support, Monty Betham and Nathan Fien. Cullen Sports director Maurice Kidd was there as well and so was New Zealand Rugby League chairman Selwyn Pearson. I took a seat at the front table with Mick. I'd been in the same room at another media conference less than a year earlier to announce I would be staying with the club after all — and now I was back to say I would definitely be going this time. It really began to hit me then that this actually was a big moment in my life. For 11 seasons I'd been a Warrior. I loved the club and loved the place. It was all I'd known as a professional footballer, and as an adult, and now I was making the most important decision of my career. I'd made a few before, like the one in late 2000 when I decided to stay with the club after Eric Watson had taken it over. It would have been understandable if

Mum and Dad with Jamie (left), Jason and me (front) on the day we were confirmed.

One of my favourite photos . . . I'm on the right with my cousin Jack and my grandfather Maunga Emery, a former Kiwi.

The Pt Chevalier No 7 breaks the line against Otahuhu. That's Awen Guttenbeil trying to keep up with me.

I was around eight here and already dreaming of playing for the Kiwis.

7 May 1997 and coming of age time but already in my third season as a first-grade footballer.

All scrubbed up for the Warriors' 1995 awards . . . Hitro Okesene was the clubman of the year, I won the rookie award, captain Dean Bell was given a special award and Tea Ropati was player of the year.

More Warriors awards and time to look sharp again . . . (above) with my old mate the Mad Butcher (Peter Leitch) at the 1999 awards dinner and (below) with the Prime TV viewers' choice award in 2001.

Photosport

The 2002 New Zealand Rugby League Awards — hanging on tight to the trophies after being named the player of the year and personality of the year.

A beautiful bride and a proud husband on the day we were married — 2 October 1999.

The Kiwis had a family day at Bondi Beach before the 2003 test against Australia . . . Awen and Tash are there while I look after Chellcey and Waiana.

Rachelle and I listen to Awen as he gives it to me at my testimonial luncheon in 2005. He'll keep.

Photosport

I'm humbled after CEO Mick Watson (left) makes me a Warriors life member at the club's 2005 NRL season launch.

Photosport

Rachelle and I gave Prime Minister Helen Clark something to cheer her up at my testimonial luncheon.

Junior Kiwis 1994 — I was captain and that's my schoolmate big Joe Vagana next to me in the front row as vice-captain. Robbie Paul is on my right and former Kiwi Gary Kemble (far left, front row) was the coach. Long-time Kiwi team-mate Nigel Vagana is sixth from left in the middle row and Danny Lima, now with Warrington, is fifth from left in the back row. Sitting in front are Zane Clarke (left) and Ben Lythe (right) who both went on to play first-grade matches for the Warriors.

New Zealand v Australia, Wellington, 2001 — Back row (from left): Ruben Wiki, Ali Lauitiiti, Jerry Seuseu, Clinton Toopi, Richard Swain, Henry Paul, Monty Betham. Middle row: George Yeisamidies (trainer), David Vaealiki, Francis Meli, Stephen Kearney, Logan Swann, David Solomona, Nigel Vagana, André Reichenbach (physio), Chris Hanna (doctor). Front row: Gerard Stokes (assistant coach), Gary Freeman (coach), Craig Smith, Nathan Cayless (captain), me, Robbie Paul, John Hutchinson (media liaison), Gordon Gibbons (manager).

I'd gone then because the club was in so much trouble, but I never regretted staying. I was so grateful to Eric for becoming involved and also to Mick for the way he'd helped me all along and especially in the way he'd assisted in making my deal with UTC possible. Right now it felt right, though. It felt right to make the break even though I wasn't relishing the idea of being the centre of attention. There were people in the room from the media that I'd dealt with a lot over the years, some I respected and some I had a slightly different attitude to. And then there were others I didn't know too much about at all. They were all there for one thing. Mick started by announcing my move:

Ladies and gentlemen, thank you for being here for what is a critical day in the history of the Vodafone Warriors.

For 11 seasons now, Stacey Jones has been the face of the Warriors. No player has done more for this club than him.

But today we're here to make an announcement about his playing future after his request for a release from his contract.

Because of his stature in the club and in the game of rugby league, it was important for us to give special consideration to Stacey's case. That's the reason why we have one of our directors here in Maurice Kidd and New Zealand Rugby League chairman Selwyn Pearson as well as Stacey's team-mates Monty Betham and Nathan Fien.

Stacey and I started a process several months ago. He wasn't certain about carrying on last year but after the season we had in 2004 it was vital that we convinced him to stay with the only NRL club he'd known.

He trained outstandingly in the off-season and looked to be in his best shape for some time in our trial matches.

But Stacey told me he sensed his time was coming to an end in the NRL. I approached the directors to inform them Stacey was also struggling with the environment here and that he wanted to have a look at opportunities outside New Zealand, not just for himself but for his family as well.

Stacey and I worked together to find a new home for him. That search took us to the French club UTC, which will join the English Super League next year. As of today, we can reveal Stacey has signed a letter of intent with UTC and we are now working through the formal details of the contract. On Stacey's request, we have agreed to let him go at the end of this 2005 season.

He holds records galore at this club, he is a life member and he is everything this club represents. After 11 years of first-grade football, we're set to lose the man most identifiable with the Warriors.

We won't have another Stacey Jones but we are well-placed to move on just the same. We have to be. This is what running a club is about.

We have a succession plan in place, which is proven by our acquisition of Nathan Fien, for instance.

To Stacey, we say thanks for everything so far — but there's still work to be done before you leave.

The coverage later of me in television news items and photographs showed me looking fairly down, I suppose. That wasn't how I felt inside. If I looked that way it was a lot to do with the occasion. I was anxious about making sure I said my bit without making a mistake. Underneath I was relieved because I was at last able to make everything clear. I can play football in front of a big crowd. That's what I do. But being in front of cameras and people to make an announcement like this is something I'll never be comfortable doing. So when Mick finished it was my turn and my hand was shaking so much holding the piece of paper with my thoughts on it:

Thanks for coming along today.

There's been a lot of speculation about my future lately. I couldn't say anything about it before because discussions were still going on about my plans to join the French club UTC next year.

Now I've agreed to terms I asked the club to bring this announcement forward so I can get on with putting all my efforts into playing my best football for the Warriors.

Because this is such a big decision for me, I've put some thoughts down on paper so please excuse me for reading them out to you.

I love the Warriors and I always will. I'm a life member and I'm really proud of that after being here since the club started in 1995.

Being a Warrior has always been really important to me but there comes a time when you know yourself that you need a change.

So right at the start of our off-season I sat down with Mick to talk about my plans.

It had been on my mind for quite a while to look at finishing up in the NRL at the end of 2005 so I told Mick I would put everything I had into the off-season, play one more year and then I'd like to move on.

I thought it was time for someone else to come in and there are plenty of players here who will step up.

Mick and I talked about it and I told him I thought my time was up in the NRL and that I wanted to move on to another opportunity and a change of lifestyle.

Asking for a release is always a special case and I really appreciate the help Mick has given me with this and with putting my deal together with UTC.

I've loved my footy with the Warriors so far this season. The guys are all brilliant to be around, I've enjoyed the new coaching team and I have always had a good relationship with this management. I'd also like to thank Monty and Nathan for being here to support me today.

This is my 11th season in the NRL. It's tough when you play in it for that long but there are other things I want to do now. I want to get away from the spotlight so I can just play football and try to have some normal time with my family. That's why I'm looking forward to going to France.

There's still plenty to do here, though. I have total faith in our coaching staff and the team. In the second half against Newcastle we showed what we're capable of and I know if we can play like that consistently we'll be up there later in the season.

I want this year to finish well and I'll do everything I can to help the team and to thank the club for what it's done for me.

Finally, I want to thank all the fans for their support and I hope you keep supporting us in what I think is going to be an exciting season.

In the media release that was sent out, Maurice Kidd also made some comments, saying the Cullen Sports directors were convinced I should be granted my wish to leave and to do so under my own terms.

'We have no wish to keep Stacey, and especially someone of his standing, against his will,' he said. 'No one can match the contribution he has made to the club in good times and bad for which we will always be appreciative. Now it's time for us to allow him to follow his wishes. He will go at the end of the season with our complete understanding and support.'

It was over — but it wasn't. The media had been told I wouldn't take questions so Mick had a few fired at him instead while I listened. That was uncomfortable but I felt a lot happier when we were able to escape from that room.

It set things off. Radio was going on about my decision, it was given lots of coverage on television news that night and then in the papers the following morning. Soon enough I was being criticised for not taking questions at the media conference. I didn't see that as such an issue but the media did and so did many of the public. They all seemed to think it meant I had something to hide. They have no idea how wrong they were. There was nothing more to this than met the eye. I've said it already and I'll say it again — I wanted to go, it was my call. It wasn't a question of being fed up with the club or anything like that. I loved playing for the Warriors. It would be fair to say, though, that some of the outside pressures had begun to wear thin. I'd been close to leaving in 2004, very close. If I'd gone then it would have been on a sour note because I wasn't happy after what had happened between Daniel Anderson and me. When he left and the effort went into trying to make me stay on, I'd agreed and didn't regret it, but now I had moved on from that. I was ready and happy to go — but only after I'd thrown everything I had into this last season with the Warriors.

I did one interview, though. I decided I wanted to talk to John Matheson from the *Sunday News* about what I'd done. The idea of doing one long interview suited me. That gave me a chance to add a few more thoughts and maybe it was that and the fact I'd given an interview that stirred things up more. There was a fair bit of scrapping going on about it between some guys in the media which I thought wasn't a good look. So much was being said and written about what I'd done and how I'd done it, even more so because I made a few comments about the media in the *Sunday News* story. As it happened, Mick had said a few things about my attitude towards the media in a radio interview, too, and that fired it up a little bit more. It just went on and on and mostly it was along the lines that I'd been forced to leave. The more it went on like that, the more I realised I should have answered questions at the conference. I regretted that in the end but I still didn't think it warranted the way some people went on.

What really got me was a column Chris Rattue wrote in the *New Zealand Herald*. He had a few cracks which I didn't believe were reasonable. I wanted to understand where he was coming from so I rang him up to have a decent chat about it. He was good about it and said he'd like to give me the right of reply. I accepted and that cleared the air a bit. Murray Deaker also asked me to come into the studio to appear on his programme on Sky Sport. I didn't want to do that but agreed to talk to him in a telephone interview instead. That might have tidied a few things up as well but I still couldn't escape the feeling people thought there was more to this than anyone was letting on. While it wasn't going to make any difference to what I would do, I still wished people had taken me on my word with this one. In some ways, though, that probably summed up why I was keen to move on.

I signed for UTC with the plan to play in two seasons in 2006 and 2007 and then see what happens. That was still ahead of me. Once the rugby league world knew what I was doing, I wanted to finish off well with the Warriors. I'd enjoyed every moment but, while I wanted to go, there was no use getting all emotional about it and I wouldn't. Part of the reason for that was the fact I would be leaving New Zealand only temporarily. I will be coming back to live. Of that I'm sure. Two seasons in France will be but a sojourn, not the destination I imagined for the end of my rugby league career after starting the game 25 years ago but, funnily enough, one of my first clubs also had a French name — Point Chevalier.

Footy for life

Soon enough I won't be running around like this anymore. When my two-year contract expires with Les Catalans I'm reasonably convinced I'll quit, at this level at least. I'll be 31, which isn't ancient but it will feel old enough after what I've been through in 13 years of first-grade rugby league.

Because I'm not a forward — and never would have been — I don't get bashed around like Awen and some of those idiots who play up front. They can have that. But I have still been bashed around enough for a little guy. I could play smart, stay out of trouble and get a couple more years out of my body — if I wanted to. I just can't see that I will. So when it all finishes in Perpignan my total playing days will span something like 27 years, nearly half of them as a first-grade player, with a total of more than 300 top-level games.

It's weird really. When I was a little kid I played rugby league the moment I was able to. I was that small you wouldn't believe. Well, maybe you would given I'm hardly a giant now. But I was tiny when I first started playing as a four-year-old and Mum thinks I might even have been as young as three. I look at the photos now and I don't know how I managed it. There's one when I first started playing with

Ponsonby-Maritime alongside my twin brothers Jamie and Jason, who are two years older than me. I was the young kid playing with the big boys and it showed. I'm not so sure I was all that worried about playing that first year. I just liked to get my gear on and play in the mud — and my goal usually was to get dirtier after the game than during it.

Most people would know exactly what I mean about tiny tots playing sport. Next time the footy season comes around, just go down to a park and have a look at the kids running around. Try to find the smallest bloke out there and then you might have an idea of what I'm talking about but, if size was an issue in that first year, it never bothered me. Mine was really a sporting life typical of so many New Zealand kids. Maybe I was a bit more obsessive about it than others but as far as I was concerned there was nothing too unusual about my liking for sport, above all rugby league and cricket. I couldn't tell you the specific posters I had on my bedroom wall now but I had plenty of teams plastered all over the place. I was one of those kids who lived out his sporting fantasies, too. They make me chuckle now when I stop to think about them, but everything was deadly serious then.

What I obviously needed were understanding parents, and Mum (Rama) and Dad (Billy) couldn't have been better about it. In a way I was almost guaranteed the chance to have a passionate interest in sport. Let's face it, the odds were fairly good in this case. Dad had played rugby union and a bit of rugby league and he was — and still is — nuts about his league. He loves the game, absolutely loves it. And Mum . . . well, that was easy. Her father is Maunga Emery and, as I found out early enough, my granddad had a decent sporting story of his own. It's not something he talks about a lot. He doesn't need to because other people do the talking for him. He started out in rugby union and played for the Maori All Blacks in the 1950s before switching to league, becoming a Kiwi from 1961 to 1966 when he played 23 tests and made the big tour to Britain and France twice. There was another league connection through the Mazzoleni family.

My uncle Dave is married to Mum's sister Trish and had a background as a hooker with Ponsonby; he later coached me, as well as acting as a manager/adviser along the way. I was certainly born into the game; about that there could be no argument.

In a country so steeped in its rugby union culture I can't quite say I never played the 15-man game but I had only a brief taste of it. I spent a year at Western Springs College in Auckland when, rather than be the nifty little bloke at halfback, I was actually a nippy guy on the wing. That was just a school deal playing union then. My sporting diet was reserved mainly for rugby league in winter and cricket in summer, although my liking for sport ran across all codes.

Growing up in central Auckland — first in Westmere and then Point Chevalier — I had two ready-made playmates in my brothers and we indulged in plenty of backyard contests. My cousin Jack would be there with us most of the time, too. At other times Jamie and Jason would be doing other things and I'd pester them to play. If they wouldn't I'd be left to my own devices, which never seemed to bother me unduly because I'd run around kicking a ball on my own, or I'd play cricket on my own. I did the things so many kids do, imagining I was this player or that player with a special liking for Alfie Langer and Gary Freeman; a few years later I'd be playing against them, and with Gary as it turned out with the Kiwis in his last year. It's strange to think it all came about after starting that way in the 1980s when I could amuse myself for any length of time living in my own little sporting world.

My real sporting world in league terms was built around three clubs, initially Ponsonby-Maritime followed by Mount Albert but mainly Point Chevalier from the age of eight. I still think the time I spent playing with Jason and Jamie, being among older players, helped me a lot. I was only young but I really believe it made a difference to me when I ended up playing with kids my own age. It made me a better player.

What I loved, too, was watching sport, especially rugby league. That's how I picked most things up, just by taking it all in. I was helped there because my grandparents had access to a satellite dish so I could go to their place to watch the Australian league coverage on Saturday and stay there the night. I well recall watching grand finals like Manly against Canberra in 1987, Balmain against Canterbury-Bankstown in 1988 and especially Canberra against Balmain in 1989, the best grand final there has ever been according to most people. That all helped me with my attitude towards playing the game and learning about it, but it wasn't just about watching games on television. I saw City-Pt Chev play a lot when I was on the sideline as a ball boy or I went to Carlaw Park on a Sunday to watch club footy there. It was fantastic. I loved it there and all the time I'd take it in. I didn't look only at halfbacks either. I studied the whole game, watching all players to see what they did.

My real growth period in playing the game came at Point Chevalier. Jason and Jamie both played senior football for City-Pt Chev and made Auckland teams, Jamie as a centre and Jason as a back-rower; they just didn't kick on. We were all in it as a family with Dad being involved as a manager in teams I played for, like the Point Chev under-17 team when Uncle Dave was the coach.

Further education in the game came at St Paul's College, where a rugby league tradition started to build while I was there. Joe and Nigel Vagana were team-mates at school and so was future Canberra winger Greg Wolfgramm, while the kick boxer Jason Suttie had played for the school before me with Francis Meli, Evarn Tuimavave and Jerome Ropati among those to follow. Dennis Marra was an important coaching influence at St Paul's and former Kiwi Sam Panapa also worked with us there. While halfback was always my position of choice I actually found myself at fullback for St Paul's for a bit, which I didn't mind too much, but I'm a great believer that it helps any young player immeasurably if he can play in the halfback's position as much as possible if that's the spot he wants to fill on a long-term basis. You need as much exposure to it as possible to be able to develop your all-round game.

Much as I revelled in rugby league, cricket was a great passion as well.

I really enjoy watching cricket now. At school it was an attraction because it worked in so well with the rugby league season. Our First XI at St Paul's was quite a way down the pecking order among Auckland schools. Put another way, we weren't that good. Joe played and Nigel was the captain. That tells you something about the quality of the side. I used to fancy myself with both bat and ball but these days I save my best cricketing performances for when I towel up Awen. He struggles against me.

Speaking of Awen, he had become a constant in rugby league and a great mate when we first started playing together for Point Chevalier at the age of 13. He was this gangling second-rower who moved from Whangarei with his family and was going to Kelston Boys' High School. We got on famously and went on to play in teams together for the next 16 years until I finished up at the Warriors to go to France. Only when he spent time as a junior with Manly were we not team-mates. In those Point Chevalier days, we weren't total angels but there's no way I was ever close to being involved in anything bad. I was lucky to be involved with blokes who all had the common goal of playing football and doing what it took.

While Awen specialised as a back-rower, it was as a halfback that I made Auckland teams through the grades as well as development sides. I was also picked as captain of the New Zealand under-17 team in 1993 — Awen and Robbie Paul were in that side — and I led the Junior Kiwis in 1994 when we beat the Australian Schoolboys in one of our two tests over there. Team-mates in that side included future Warriors team-mates Joe and Nigel Vagana and Robbie as well as Zane Clarke and Ben Lythe; also in that side was Danny Lima, the former Roosters, Canberra and Manly forward who's now with Warrington in the English Super League.

Whenever I went away with Auckland teams, Mum and Dad plus Dave and Trish would always come. I made trips to Australia with Auckland Development teams — when John Ackland was the coach — and I also had a huge trip when I was about 16 with what was a New Zealand development side. Coached by Stan Martin, we went to

England and had a great experience there. We were all billeted with New Zealanders who were playing there. I was looked after by Shane Cooper who was then with St Helens while guys like Tea Ropati, Frano Botica and Sam Panapa were also involved in taking in players.

We had to do a lot of fundraising for that tour and I was the youngest in a team that also included future Newcastle and Warriors prop Jason Temu, another Warrior-to-be Willie Poching and Greg Ashby, who played a lot of footy for Glenora. The tour itself was well organised but the football aspect was a little loose.

As a rugby league career began to take some shape and certainly become important to my future, my personal life also did the same when I met Rachelle. She provided some real structure for me and within a few years we would become husband and wife as well as having two beautiful daughters in Chellcey and Waiana, with a third child on the way in late 2005.

Naturally, my parents have had a huge influence on me. What Mum and Dad have done is a reflection of what I've wanted to do and to become. In my time I've bought a few cars but I've never gone overboard. I've just been smart. I could have done better in terms of how much money I might have earned from the game but I could have done a lot worse, too. I've been happy to live comfortably without going over the top. I haven't got into any businesses, investing in some property instead. When I finish playing, we're not going to live the high life. That's not really my style. I just want to enjoy it, to be able to spend a lot more time at our family beach place in Doubtless Bay way up north. It's a place we went to all the time, ever since I can remember. Dad's parents have got a farm there which we used to love going to, too; a great experience for city kids like us.

But the common thread throughout has been rugby league, of course, and while my football education went along in leaps when I was at St Paul's, I'd say I just got there with my school work. It suffered through the various commitments I had. I wouldn't claim to be a bright student but I completed my fifth- and sixth-form years successfully before conflicts got in the way in my seventh-form year.

By then the Warriors had become a reality and all I could think of was playing for the club at some stage. It really was the best feeling for young footballers knowing we were going to have our own Winfield Cup club in Auckland.

The first significant chance I had to do something about it came when the Warriors organised under-17 and under-19 trials at Jack Colvin Park, the home of the Te Atatu league club in West Auckland. Warriors coach John Monie, CEO Ian Robson and reserve-grade coach Frank Endacott were all there to run the rule over the players and afterwards they gave out junior scholarships to about 10 of us. Henry and Robbie Paul were both in that group along with Joe, Nigel, Logan Swann and Gus Malietoa Brown. Out of that you received some money for schooling as well as some gear then, early in 1995, we were signed up on proper lower-level contracts. In reserve grade we were on $100 a game and $200 a win and every Thursday it would be pay day, which was something to look forward to. If you made it to first-grade, you were looking at $600 a win and $200 a loss so it was all looking great to me.

This was no longer my little rugby league fantasy world; this was footy for life.

Show me the Monie

As an 18-year-old not long out of St Paul's College, it was a lot to take in. Billy and Rama Jones' little boy was still reasonably little — I couldn't do much about that — but I was suddenly in the very big league. Even so, nothing could have prepared me for what I saw on Friday, 10 March 1995.

A year earlier I'd been playing for the Auckland Vulcans in the Lion Red Cup when a few hundred people represented a big crowd. And before that I was just a young bloke playing club football for my Point Chevalier club. So much had changed since then and changed in a hurry but it's that night you keep going back to whenever you talk about the Warriors.

A little more than 10 years later, I found myself going over it all again. The club decided to make a big deal out of marking the 10th anniversary of the Warriors' debut in the old Winfield Cup competition. Not by doing it on the same date or near the same date but by celebrating it against the original opponents. Ever since the club started life, the match-up that always defines the Warriors is every game we play against Brisbane, especially at Ericsson Stadium. They're just the best contests, always special.

The 2005 event couldn't have been much better. We had replica original strips made, the Polynesian drummers were in residence again and, with Steve Price out injured, I had the thrill of leading the team onto the field from the tunnel used that first night. Looking on and being made a fuss of were eight of the 1995 originals — Phil Blake, Whetu Taewa, Tea Ropati, Gene Ngamu, Gavin Hill, Duane Mann, Tony Tatupu and Tony Tuimavave. We were wound up for the occasion — everyone was revelling in it — and when it was all over, we were able to bask in the kind of result we all wanted, a 30–18 victory. It was just a great day . . .

But back to 10 March 1995, and the night the Auckland Warriors — as we were known then — arrived on the rugby league scene. I'd had an early taste of what this Warriors thing was all about, running out onto Ericsson Stadium just before 6 p.m. for the reserve-grade curtain-raiser against the Broncos. Frank Endacott was our coach and the captain was Willie Poching, better known these days as a long-serving player for the Leeds Rhinos in the English Super League. Our side contained a few players who had been Kiwis or were soon to play for their country like fullback Peter Edwards, centre Mike Dorreen, props Simon Angell and Joe Vagana, hooker Syd Eru and back-rowers Jason Mackie and Logan Edwards. We faced a Brisbane side including Paul Hauff, the fullback who never played for Australia again after making his debut in their 1991 test defeat by the Kiwis. Future Kiwi — and Kangaroo — Tonie Carroll was in the centres, the seasoned Terry Matterson was at loose forward and league great in the making Shane Webcke was one of the props.

We gave the night a decent kick-start before the real entertainment started in the shape of an amazing pre-match show and then the main event. In fact, we were really happy with ourselves after walking off with a 36–14 victory to our name. For me it was a good night personally with a try and six goals — then I couldn't wait to get showered, dressed and back out there sitting in the stand to take everything in. Like the other 31,000 people there, I was blown away by the night, the only negative being the 25–22 defeat, and even that didn't feel so bad at the time. This was the Winfield Cup and I wanted more.

Coach John Monie and Ian Robson had signed me up with the Warriors originally, upgrading me from a junior scholarship I was on. Henry Paul was one of that junior group as well until he went to Wakefield Trinity for an off-season. Next thing Wigan had an interest in him and, for whatever reason, the Warriors decided to let him go in a swap for prop Andy Platt. That was a strange one. If they'd kept Henry, the Warriors would have had his younger brother Robbie, too. Who knows how things might have worked out with those two at the club, say Robbie at standoff and Henry at fullback. I don't think John had any idea then just how good Henry and Robbie could be. It's a shame we never found out.

After that first night, I ended up sitting on the interchange bench for a few matches. In those days, first-grade teams were named with two fresh reserves and the coach would add six to eight players from the reserve-grade match to join the bench. You still used four replacements — apart from the time we slipped up and used a fifth against Western Suburbs — but two of them had to be the fresh reserves while any two of the others on the bench made up the third and fourth. The call could be made on the run, depending on injuries and so on. What John would usually do was to pick 17 players, in other words including two from the reserve-grade side, but he would tell only 15 players that they were in. The other two had to play at least half a game in reserve grade to be able to play for the first-grade side.

In 1995 Bob Lanigan was working for us on the sideline on match days. He'd be telling you to get up and warm up every 15 minutes. He'd say: 'Righto, boys, get up and have a run. Stace, you're on in five minutes.' You'd have half a team running up and down the sideline because the bench would have as many as 10 players on it. I could hear John Monie on the walkie-talkie saying: 'Stacey's on in five minutes . . . but hold off, just wait, just wait!' This kept happening game after game. I'd be up and Bob would say: 'You're on next set . . . no, no. Come back.' There'd be five minutes to go and you wouldn't make it onto the field. This happened fairly much the same for five matches on end and I thought I was never going to make it onto the field. In one of those reserve-grade games we played Manly-Warringah and one of the players was familiar. It took me a while to figure out that the guy underneath the curly hair — when he had hair — was none other than Awen. He wished he'd never come that day because we smashed his mob 48–0. That was another one he didn't come close to winning.

By the seventh round we were at Parramatta Stadium playing the Eels. I'd had a run in reserve grade and we'd won by plenty — and there I was sitting on the bench for the top side again, still thinking I wouldn't get on. I wasn't sure whether I enjoyed being in with a chance of playing first grade, not when you played reserve grade and then sat out there for a whole game without coming close to being used. I can't remember but I suppose I would have preferred to have a shower, get dressed and then go back out to watch our top side. Anyway, I was out there this day — 23 April — and things were going well for us and it looked like I'd go unused once again. Suddenly it was all on. I hadn't even warmed up and Bob said: 'Stace, you're on!' I seem to recall Gene Ngamu was injured so I rushed to get my tracksuit off and on I went. I had only about five minutes, scored a try, kicked a conversion, got a cut and had to go to the blood bin. I never made it back on. And what do I remember of the try? Phil Blake put a kick through, I raced after it and he was about to dive on it when I dived in front of him and got there first. I said: 'Oh, sorry, Phil.' But he was happy for me. He'd scored a few tries in his career by then and could probably afford to let me have one. We were winning by plenty then and went on to thrash the Eels 40–4.

I had the next two games against the Roosters and Newcastle sitting on the bench again without getting on the field but, after the ninth round, everything about my rugby league world changed. The first-grade side followed the win over the Eels with what was a third successive win in beating the Roosters, only to crash badly — as we did a few times in 1995 — with a 48–6 loss to Newcastle, still one of the worst in the club's history. That led to John making all sorts of changes to the side for our next match against Cronulla, again on the road.

I had no idea I was part of the grand plan, although I do recall someone — and I think it was Bob Hall, the Warriors' coaching and development manager — asking me after the Newcastle match how I felt about playing No 6. No worries, I said. The following week I looked at the team up on the board — you weren't told face to face about selection when Monie was coach — and my name was there to wear the No 6 jersey. No one had dropped any hints and I was naturally charged up to see it. Was I ready for this? Who could say? I'd had just a few minutes of first-grade football and a handful of matches for the reserves and now I was picked to start in the top side.

The team was so different to what John had been running until then. Apart from my selection, Brandy (Greg Alexander) was moved from halfback to fullback, John Kirwan had his first start on one wing, Mike Dorreen also made the run-on side for the first time in the centres, Gene Ngamu moved from standoff to halfback, Tony Tuimavave came back into the back row, Syd Eru took over at hooker from Duane Mann and Andy Platt was in for Se'e Solomona at prop. That was a lot of selection movement. One of the other changes was Richie Blackmore's inclusion on the bench after just arriving home from England.

While I made my debut against Parramatta, it's the Cronulla match I remember more as my real start in the Winfield Cup, mainly because I was in the starting side and was on for the whole match rather than coming on for a few minutes off the bench. It was a crucial match for the club, too, really crucial for our season after such an embarrassing defeat. It was an even bigger day back home, Mother's Day for a start — and that's always important — but also the day Team New Zealand lifted the America's Cup.

Ours wasn't quite as momentous as winning the cup but it was a significant one just the same as we came back from 18–14 down to level things at 18–18 with a Sean Hoppe try — and then a few minutes later I was able to nail a field goal for the all-important advantage. Hitro Okesene finished it off with a late try to give us a well-merited 23–18 win and a great personal outcome for me in the top grade. I loved every minute of it.

STACEY JONES

That's how things really started for me with the Warriors and everything took off after that. I played every match from then on right through to the last match of the 1999 season against Western Suburbs — 100 matches straight before the sequence was broken but it's that first season that sticks for pure excitement. Just to put your training gear on was a huge buzz and the whole city was up for the Warriors, most of the country actually. It wasn't that long ago that I'd been watching guys like Greg Alexander playing for Penrith in the competition I'd always dreamed of playing in — and now I was in it training and playing with Brandy. We had some decent names in our squad apart from him, too, like Dean Bell, John Kirwan, Sean Hoppe, Phil Blake, Tea Ropati, Stephen Kearney, Andy Platt, Richie Blackmore and Duane Mann. Denis Betts and Frano Botica also joined the squad once their commitments with Wigan had finished. For a young guy it was a fantastic opportunity and that's the way I always looked at it.

I was also lucky I had Frank Endacott as our reserve-grade coach in that first year. He was the biggest influence on me then, helping me adapt to this new life where so much was going on at a time when I was still so young and inexperienced. He was always keen to talk and give advice. I also had a lot of support from Steve and Hitro. They were great to me.

Also great was some of the football we played in a season noted for a share of spectacular wins and, if I'm honest, a few spectacular duds. While we scratched around for the first half of the season we picked up some form in the second half by stringing together victories over teams that might have been seen as less fancied but were still sides you had to beat if you were to be in contention. So, we had to be pleased when we put together consecutive wins over Western Suburbs 16–12, South Sydney 38–20, Gold Coast 44–16, Western Reds 34–10, South Queensland 22–10 and North Queensland 28–10. To say the place was buzzing then would have been an understatement. There really was a feeling we were on to something — but just as we were getting fairly excited about our achievements we ran into St George. Imagine this. There's a crowd of 28,973 crammed into Ericsson Stadium, all expectant as we try to make it seven wins on end. This was going to be the test of how good we were. So, what a letdown it turned out to be — the Dragons absolutely smashed us 47–14 in a match many people still recall for an amazing try scored by a young Gorden Tallis.

We weren't out of it but that result left us needing to win two of our last three to be sure of a top-eight spot. We managed only one and finished with a limp effort against Brisbane when we were done 42–6. That left us on 24 points, equal eighth with North Sydney and the Roosters but with an inferior points-for-and-against differential, which really fell to pieces with the performance against the Broncos.

I'd started out as an absolute novice, not expecting to make any sort of ground on established players, yet I'd finished the season starting in the club's last 13 matches straight, 14 appearances all up counting my interchange debut. Throw in five tries, nine goals and two field goals — 40 points in all — and it left me in a bit of a daze. More so because, by then, I was also a real professional footballer earning money that was light years better than it had been when the season started.

That was because I was part of the set-up when the war broke out, the conflict, that is, between News Ltd and their Super League vision taking on the Australian Rugby League (ARL), the establishment. It all began to not so much develop as explode the day we played the Bears at North Sydney Oval, on April Fool's Day, as it happened. What a mind-boggling time that was, although I wasn't anywhere near the centre of the action then being such a young player. The big boys were into that. I had no idea what was going on.

What I do remember was the senior players, 15 or so of them, going to a meeting at John Monie's place in Titirangi when we got back from the North Sydney trip. A day later John told a group of us we had a meeting at a hotel in the city with a lawyer representing Super League or the News Ltd people. Apart from me, there were Joe Vagana, Tony Tuimavave, Tony Tatupu and maybe one or two others. John talked to me a bit about it, not that much, but I always remember him saying: 'Don't miss the boat, Stace.' I wasn't sure what he meant. I had Mum and Dad with me and, when we saw Joe come out of the meeting with a huge smile, we thought this must be really good.

We went in and I soon found out what John meant. I'd signed with the Warriors for only about $3000, which was fairly standard for younger players — but suddenly I was being offered $60,000 plus a $25,000 loyalty payment. You can imagine what that does to an 18-year-old. I signed fairly quickly. After all, that comment about not missing the boat was fresh in my mind. When I did sign, Dad was quick to tell me not to waste the money, not to spend it on things I didn't need, like a car or something else. I took his advice. I put the money in the bank — and then took it out a week later to buy a car; well, around $15,000 anyway.

I look back at it now and realise I should have held off signing in such a hurry. Steve Kearney had also tried to help me out with some advice but really it was all too exciting and I had no hesitation signing a new Super League deal with the Warriors. By then I had played just a few reserve-grade games so what else would you do when you were 18 and someone was offering you money 30 times better than what you're on? A couple of days later I was questioning myself. Graham Lowe was tied up with North Queensland then and he called to offer me $200,000 to sign for the Cowboys! It was too late by then. I'd basically been shafted, especially when I heard the money some other guys were on. Later a whole lot of the salaries were published and even Awen was there listed as being paid $150,000. No wonder he always believes he's better than me! I certainly missed out then. Did I regret that? A little, maybe, but I was still happy with my lot.

For a young bloke, this professional business was looking good to me. We enjoyed the good life, I must say. We'd go to restaurants and Ian Robson would have the credit card out and let us order anything. We lived like kings with guys ordering up crayfish, some having three main courses and buying expensive bottles of wine. I don't know what happened to having a steak and a couple of beers. It was unreal. The money that was basically being wasted was incredible but it didn't seem to bother Ian, and the boys weren't about to complain.

We'd finished that first year reasonably well I guess, although the season wasn't as good as it should have been. We had a very strong squad with a mix of top-class players from Australia and England; what I'm saying is that the ability was there to make the top eight without any stress. All through the side there was talent and experience in all key positions with the core strength provided by Dean Bell, Greg Alexander, Steve Kearney, Phil Blake, Denis Betts, Tea Ropati, Sean Hoppe, Andy Platt, Duane Mann, Richie Blackmore and Frano Botica while John Kirwan had plenty of top-level sporting experience he could offer from his All Black days. While some of them were later starters after coming out from England, and injury and form also played a part, a squad of that quality should have been further up the points table. The fact we weren't probably had a bit to do with the newness of it all, including issues like the constant travel involved.

On a playing level, I probably didn't learn too much in terms of adding to my game that year. I gained in experience, of course, just through being able to play alongside so many good players in a tough competition, but I remained much the same as a player, doing nothing more than playing my normal game, which was the advice I'd been given by John. He didn't want to put a heap of pressure on me. He wanted to see me supporting, backing up and having a go whenever it was on. I wasn't filling a role or creating or organising plays then and I thought it was great that I was able to settle into first-grade football that way rather than being asked to do too much in what was a crucial position. We did, after all, have Brandy and Gene in the team who could run the show.

It was a little bit intimidating being out there with so many seasoned players with big reputations, especially for someone who was naturally shy like me. That didn't last too long, though, because the guys all made it easy. Steve was great to play with. He knew it was hard for a young guy coming into the team so he helped by telling me what he wanted by giving me clear directions. I appreciated that.

In some ways it was probably more challenging coming into the Kiwis later in the year than it was playing for the Warriors. In the

Kiwis, some of the guys were more demanding in terms of what they expected of me on the field. Blokes like Quentin Pongia and Tony Iro would order me around but that was the best way for me to learn. You need to be spoken to sternly, or forcefully — just not yelled at. I think that's the difference. It was that approach of bringing me along that made it a lot easier for me playing for the Warriors and then New Zealand.

John Monie was probably a little difficult for me to get a line on as a coach because I was young and so new to it all. I was too concerned about doing my own job to worry about that. He didn't talk a lot, certainly not to me, and he wasn't the sort of bloke a young guy like me would go and have a beer with. With John, the major thing was that he gave me the opportunity to play first-grade football and I will always be grateful for that.

Off the field I got on well with Gene, Brandy and Hitro. We'd always be down at Park in the Bar in the city after a match at home. That used to be the place to go to then. Even on Wednesday night before a game we'd go out, and not just for a couple of beers. That's the way it was then. You wouldn't think twice. You'd turn up to training a bit seedy the next day but you'd get through it. There was also very little trouble then with any of our players as I recall it. Players are far more professional these days but there seem to be more behaviour issues because the media's always out there looking for them. You just can't really relax the way we could in the earlier years. I understand the need for that. The public have a high expectation of us in terms of our behaviour and standards; at the same time, we also like to have fun when we can. With everything, it comes back to balance again.

Our squad was tweaked for the 1996 season with John making a few signings. Kiwi forward Mark Horo returned to New Zealand after stints with Parramatta and Western Suburbs, Awen joined us from Manly and two more former All Blacks, Marc Ellis and Mark Carter, were also signed. With JK still there, that gave us three big rugby union names, although the initiations for the two newest ones were markedly different. Ellis lasted longer with the game and also made the Kiwis but Carter returned to union after 1996. Otherwise, we had much the same playing roster, although a few had moved on, including Frano Botica and Dean Bell, who was such an inspirational captain in his one season with us before he retired. We'd miss him, of that there was no doubt.

Our off-season training then didn't differ that much from what we've done in that area in more recent times. There were the usual strength and skills sessions as well as a lot of aerobic work at places like One Tree Hill, while we also had camps where the partners went along, first at Hopuhopu and then Pakatoa Island leading into the 1996 year. Everything was still being done with a fair amount of style and no little expense.

The 1996 season was fairly edgy because the Super League v ARL conflict was building. The intention had been to go straight into the Super League competition in 1996. In fact, the Warriors had signed Matthew Ridge from Manly — an ARL club — and he'd trained with us all summer in the expectation of being able to play for us. Ultimately, it couldn't happen and Ridgey returned to play the year out with Manly, and win a premiership as well. It was messy at the start of the season. Super League players were all on strike, refusing to play for their clubs. We were down to play Brisbane and the Warriors scratched together teams from two local clubs to play if required; they didn't have to because Brisbane forfeited and we picked up two easy competition points.

We went well enough early on, beating Illawarra twice, North Sydney and Parramatta, only to go cold with four successive losses before picking up again by beating Penrith, Western Suburbs, South Sydney and Gold Coast. We had difficulties, though, with the top sides and our form away from home wasn't too encouraging, so we finished much the same as we had in 1995. I felt I'd grown, appearing in all 21 matches we played — and scoring six tries — and I'd again been able to function without too many demands being placed on me.

By the time the 1997 season came around, rugby league was in a rocky state as Super League and News Ltd went out on their own, leaving the ARL to run a separate competition. It wasn't at all good for the game. Of course it wasn't. But this was coming as we all knew it would. There'd been an outbreak of war as such in 1995 and a compromise was needed in 1996 to keep a combined competition going.

Things were also uneasy inside the Warriors, the DB Bitter Warriors as we were in those days. The person under the greatest strain was Ian Robson. We didn't know much of what was happening inside the boardroom but it became obvious Ian was in trouble, apparently over expenditure. In time the board ran out of patience with him and he was sacked early in the year. Not that long after, John Monie would join him.

When you look at it now, John's coaching record was very reasonable. I'll confess I didn't know this off the top of my head but I had some research done to check things out and John's winning percentage was exactly 50 per cent after 26 wins and 26 losses. Frank Endacott, Mark Graham and Tony Kemp all finished with records below 40 per cent and only Daniel Anderson could top John's effort with 51 wins from his 92 matches, which meant we won 55 per cent of our matches when he was coach.

But back in the club's early years, John's record ultimately wasn't good enough. I suppose with so much put into starting the club up and building a squad — and, compared to other clubs, we had some really good players — there were expectations of a better return. We were very close to the top eight in 1995 and we were right in it for eighth place again in 1996. The point was we didn't succeed and then things started going wrong early on when we joined the nine other sides in Super League's Telstra Cup in 1997.

Obviously, the overall strength of both the Super League and ARL competitions wasn't there. Of the 10 teams in our competition, there were a couple of new clubs like the Adelaide Rams and the Hunter Mariners. We also had the Western Reds and the North Queensland Cowboys who were battling, which left us, Brisbane, Cronulla, Canberra, the Bulldogs and Penrith.

We should have been in there competing with the best sides but the season was a bit of a struggle from the start. We lost 14–2 to Brisbane first up, beat Hunter at home, took a pounding from the Sharks and lost to Adelaide in a shocker at Ericsson. Wins against Penrith and then Canberra put us in better shape but then we lost to Hunter. I remember I had a good game against the Raiders and did quite a bit of media work in the week after but then had a fairly ordinary match against Hunter. So, in front of the team, John said: 'It looks like you've been reading too much of your own press, Stace.' He tried to joke to me about it with the boys there but pulled me aside later and said: 'Come on, Stace, let's get back on the horse this week.' Actually, things didn't work out so well after that because we were well beaten by the Bulldogs next time out, giving us just three wins from eight as we headed towards the Anzac test. That wasn't too flash.

Sean Hoppe, Gene Ngamu, Grant Young, Syd Eru, Stephen Kearney, Tea Ropati, Joe Vagana and I were all involved in the test and the day after we had to fly up to Townsville for our next Telstra Cup match against the Cowboys. Gene had already read in the paper or heard from someone that he was going to be dropped for the game and that Shane Endacott would be taking his place at standoff. So, he wasn't feeling too good about things when we had a team meeting that night. After talking to us, John said: 'Oh, Gene, I'd like to have a word with you.' And Gene bit back: 'And I'd like to have a word with *you*!' Nothing changed after their discussion. Gene started the match on the bench.

The Cowboys were on the bottom of the ladder but they led 14–4 at halftime and finished up winning 30–22 to give us our third loss on end. I can't say I was aware things were about to change, and change very quickly, but it later emerged that DB Breweries, our major sponsor, wasn't pleased with our performances and some serious questions were being asked in the boardroom.

At the same time, there seemed to be something going on while we were in Townsville. That night there was actually a fight, a blue between a few senior players — no names — which might have had something to do with John. I'm not sure about that but there was some unease around the place.

We were back in Auckland the following day and by Tuesday John had gone. The CEO Bill MacGowan came into the meeting room — John wasn't there — and told us Frank had been appointed the new first-grade coach. The first thing Frank said was: 'Okay, boys, no training today. We're going down to the Trident Tavern.' That was how he started out, the good old-fashioned way of going to the pub to have a couple of beers. That was happy Frank. You wouldn't have expected anything else from him.

Happy Frank

Out went one coach, in came a new one and within 18 months I'd be shaking hands with another one yet again. I guess those were the times when the Warriors' rollercoaster really started to roll. As a club, we were up and down all over the place, both on the field and off it. I was part of it for 11 years but it rarely affected what I wanted to do, which was simply to play football.

John Monie had gone after what was actually a reasonably successful time as coach in results terms. Some of the senior players of the time might disagree but I didn't think he created a bad atmosphere at the club or anything like that. I know there were also comments that he had difficulty working with Polynesian players; again I wasn't convinced there was a real issue there.

If there were theories about those two areas when John was coach there wouldn't be with Frank. After having him as reserve-grade coach and then in charge of the Kiwis I knew he would create a happy environment — that came naturally to him — and working with the Pacific Island boys certainly wasn't a problem because he'd done that his whole coaching life. And it's true, the season and a half with him didn't seem to change the image of the man we all call Happy Frank.

Unfortunately, results didn't change either. Frank came into our Telstra Cup campaign in late April 1997, trying to break a run of three straight losses; a few weeks later that had grown to seven in a row, which is still a club record, although we later equalled that twice. First up under Frank was a loss to Brisbane followed by the same against Canberra, Perth and Penrith. What we did have that season, though, was a welcome interlude, a Super League initiative that ultimately didn't work so well but one that I'll never forget.

Under Super League, there was an effort to spice the game up in a number of ways, some of which worked and some of which didn't. The idea of video referees came out of Super League — something even rugby union has taken on since — while the 40/20 kick was another invention from that time along with a number of other rule changes. The English Super League still has most of them. One that didn't stick down here and one I couldn't quite figure out whether I liked was the rule that the team that had just scored restarted play each time. Apart from that, the playing strips were completely different, with the jerseys having the players' surnames on the back of them.

There were also new ideas on the competition side. As a counter to the ARL's State of Origin series, we had a Super League tri series involving sides from New South Wales, Queensland and New Zealand and another new idea — sadly not continued — was the World Club Challenge. It pitted each of the 10 Super League clubs against the English Super League teams (the game in Britain was totally Super League, not split down the middle as it was in Australia). The format was a bit odd in that teams from the Southern Hemisphere played only against English Super League teams, so we took on St Helens, Bradford and Warrington in England and then, later in the season, those three sides travelled to play us in New Zealand. The top four English sides then met the top four Australasian ones in the quarter-finals — two played in England and two down here — before we got down to the semi-finals and the final. Not surprisingly, none of the English sides reached the last four.

Whatever the merits of the World Club Challenge, it was great for us because as a team we had the chance to tour. When you travel with the Warriors, it's usually a case of flying to Australia one day, playing the next and then flying home the next morning. In 1997, we finished up being away for about five weeks, first flying to Perth to play the Western Reds then on to England for the three matches there before returning home via Australia for another Telstra Cup match against Penrith. The start and the end weren't good. We lost to the Perth Reds and to the Panthers but we loved the trip.

It wasn't like being with the Kiwis when you'd be put up in some good spots. We stayed out of town near Wigan. It wasn't luxury but we had a fantastic time; we had a game every weekend and just enjoyed the experience of being on tour.

One issue there was our transport. While we had a couple of people-mover-type vehicles to take us to training sessions or whatever else we had to do, there wasn't enough room for everyone. So Gene and I bought a little car, a VW Golf it was. It was being advertised for £250 and Gene and I went to see the woman who was selling it, taking Tony Tuimavave and Matthew Ridge with us. Tony was our mechanic to check the car out and Ridgey was our negotiator. Who else would you expect for that job? And it's easy to imagine how he went about his work, too. Put it this way, he was a fairly aggressive negotiator. Tony did his bit as well. He took the car for a drive and told the owner the steering was a bit off and that a few other things weren't so good either. The end result was Gene and I had the car for £150.

It was a terrible car. Fumes poured inside it and you needed to wear masks whenever you drove it. In the end we trashed it on our last night. We left it in the car park and every time anyone walked past it they'd put the boot into it or something like that. It was a total mess the next morning and a truck with a crane had to be brought in to take it away.

On the football field we had a much better time of it, too. We didn't know what to expect when we came up against St Helens at Knowsley Road but it all went our way as we ran away 42–14.

A week later we had what we regarded as the test match of the tour against Bradford, then the top side in England. When we had Syd Eru ordered off we were facing a battle having to play most of the match a man short. With 10 minutes to go the Bulls led 16–14 but Gene put Paul Staladi in six minutes from time to give us a 20–16 win. In our third game we took on a Warrington side that included New Zealanders Nigel Vagana, Willie Swann and Kelly Shelford but won easily 56–28.

After a long flight to Australia, we couldn't carry on with the new-found form when we took on Penrith in the Telstra Cup, although we did recover from a 24–6 deficit to eventually lose just 26–22. Despite the loss, it was clear we had gained some confidence from being in England, even though the opposition was generally of an inferior standard to what we'd been used to. And in our last five matches of the regular season, that confidence showed through as we beat Cronulla (Frank's first win in the competition) and Adelaide, lost to the Bulldogs and then finished with wins over Perth and North Queensland. In between, we had another three matches in the World Club Challenge when the English teams travelled to play us at home. Three more wins came our way, huge ones against Bradford (64–14) and St Helens (70–6) but only 16–4 over Warrington in Christchurch in the coldest conditions I've ever played in. Unfortunately, that result cost us a home semi-final so we headed to Brisbane in early October. A win there would have set up a final at Ericsson Stadium but the Broncos came back from 16–10 down to beat us 22–16.

The schedule that season was a bit jumbled, though, because we were actually back in test mode before completing the World Club Challenge. The second test against Australia had been scheduled for 26 September, just six days after the Super League grand final. That meant eight of us from the Warriors were back together with the Kiwis — and still with Frank as our coach — to play a test at North Harbour Stadium for the first time. The Aussies had won 34–22 on Anzac Day but this turned into one of the best experiences of my career, as much because I had the satisfaction of my first test win over Australia but also because the quality of our effort was sensational.

We led only 10–6 at halftime but then completely overwhelmed Australia. Syd Eru scored twice and I also had two tries courtesy of two great balls from Steve Kearney. Richie Blackmore had a huge game coming home from Leeds, so did many of the other guys and we finished with a 30–12 win. There'd be future success against Australia but that night was a decent feeling.

The World Club Challenge semi-finals and final that followed closed the book on Super League in our part of the world. By the next year the two factions were back together as peace was reached. There's no doubt the split hurt the game but I also think it needed to happen to enable the players to be better rewarded for their part in rugby league. While the wounds are probably still healing, the competition under the National Rugby League — the NRL — is now so much better. Super League played a role in that with a lot of new ideas. The money paid to players has come down a lot from that time, and it needed to, but it's just a shame there was so much damage along the way.

The 1997 year had been notable for having Matthew Ridge as a team-mate at club level for the first time. I'd already played with him for the Kiwis and he'd trained with us leading up to the 1996 season before finally lining up with us in 1997. You couldn't wish for a better team-mate in terms of his sheer competitiveness. A lot of players didn't like him because they thought he was a bit too boisterous but I didn't have any difficulty with him. I think he was good for us, to be honest.

While Frank had the happy tag he wasn't like that all the time. He felt losses like any coach would but there's no doubt there was a happier feel around the place. I don't think some of the younger players warmed to him so much, though, because he was so loyal to the guys he knew. He spent a lot of time with them and the young blokes found it difficult to break in sometimes. That's the way Frank was, though.

Like Kempy a few years later, Frank inherited a squad and could really only try to make the most of a difficult situation. He made progress but we'd need further improvement to be contenders when the new 20-team competition started in 1998. With that many sides, the play-offs were opened up to the top 10 sides, which ought to have given us more of a chance of playing finals football at last.

We benefited from a few signings, Frank securing one of his favourite sons Quentin Pongia from Canberra while we were able to bring in Kevin Iro and Tyran Smith in the fallout from Super League folding. Also back with the Warriors after just one year with Warrington was Nigel Vagana. We had a few who moved on as well. Denis Betts finished his contract early, Phil Blake wasn't given a new contract, Marc Ellis went early in the 1998 season — heading back to rugby union — Mark Horo ended his career and Hitro Okesene was no longer a Warrior. Again there was a reasonable turnover of players.

As I've already mentioned, there's another issue that has cropped up with the Warriors year after year, and it seemed to chase John Monie around. It's that old one about the large number of Polynesian players we have and the belief that some coaches haven't been able to work with them. That's such a stupid argument and one which doesn't wash with me. The Polynesian boys are one of our greatest strengths with their skill levels, their athleticism, strength and pace. What we need is a mixture at the club to ensure there's a balance in the type of players we have. I think a lot of the Pacific Island boys have it so easy in junior football in New Zealand where, with their size, they can overwhelm sides at will and don't often find themselves in positions where they have to grind out wins. Ali Lauitiiti was an obvious case. When he came into the club you could tell all he'd had to do was attack and run with the ball.

We had coaching problems as well then — and still do — and that's a big part of it. In Australia, kids are taught the basic skills and have them drummed into them again and again. We don't do that anywhere near as well. The Australian coaching systems are way superior to

Will it go over? Yes, it does. In my first full match for the Warriors, I land a vital field goal against Cronulla in 1995.

You can't see his perm, but that's a curly-haired Awen Guttenbeil trying to stop my progress in my Kiwi test debut against Tonga at the World Cup in 2000.

Frank Endacott, my best Kiwi coach, celebrates with me after beating Great Britain in 1996.

David Peachey tries to hold me and Alfie Langer moves in to help in the Kiwis' first Super League test against Australia on Anzac Day 1997. We lost that one.

When you've just swamped Australia 30–12, why wouldn't you drench yourselves in the sponsor's product? We certainly did at North Harbour Stadium in 1997.

The big Super League 'S' on the jersey was the sign of the times in 1997. That's Hunter Mariners forward Willie Poching, a former Warrior, coming after me.

David Furner tries to chase me down in our 1998 clash against Canberra. What about the red shorts?

Test time against the Kangaroos at North Harbour Stadium in 1998.

Halfback on halfback as I take on Australia's Brett Kimmorley in the 1999 Tri Nations series at Ericsson Stadium.

The 1999 Tri Nations series is over after breaking my arm when we played Tonga.

A night not to be remembered — after the haka we were savaged 52–0 by Australia in the 2000 Anzac Test and captain Richie Barnett (right) ended the match with a dreadful injury.

Disbelief, dejection and humiliation were all wrapped into one as I try to take in the reality of our shocking loss to Australia in 2000. It was the worst experience of my whole career.

A bit of blood is spilled for the Warriors' cause but there's a winning smile this time.

The red strip was given an airing against the Bulldogs in 2000. We won this one 24–12.

ours and you see it all the time in their young players when they come through. We have the raw skill and talent but it often needs a lot of work to get those players to where they need to be. I'd say that has improved over the 11 years but there's still a big gap in what we should be doing, and some of this comes back to relationships between the Warriors, the Auckland Rugby League and the New Zealand Rugby League. We haven't been doing enough to help with coaching — by that I mean the players — and we should be doing more. In the first couple of years we did quite a lot of that work with players and schools around Auckland but there hasn't been anywhere near enough for a long time. We have to get back to that and I'm sure we will, especially now someone like John Ackland is involved in the development area.

Our greatest concerns in 1998 were on the field, though, and I'd have to say not a lot improved. We were fairly much the same old Warriors at that point. After nine rounds we had won only twice; we showed some improvement to win seven of our last 15 matches — including a stunning match when we beat Melbourne 24–21 after the hooter — but 15th in a 20-team competition and finishing eight points outside the play-offs wasn't too flash. If there was an issue, it was the fact we seemed to have trouble putting away some of the lesser sides — an opening-round loss to South Sydney, 24–18, was one example while Western Suburbs beat us 18–16, we were embarrassed 31–18 by Gold Coast, Adelaide pipped us 22–20 and we were beaten a second time, 20–18, by the Rabbitohs.

That Melbourne match really was something else. We were trailing 21–18 when Quentin Pongia executed a one-on-one strip with only seconds left, we put up a bomb and Tony Tatupu grabbed the winner. I also remember that trip because it was Monty Betham's first time coming away with us when he travelled as 18th man; he was my roomie and he had to pack my bags the day after because I was a bit under the weather.

That was a bright spot in an ordinary year, although it should be pointed out that there were some concerns off the field for the club by the end of the season as well. As we limped home with three straight losses, the final one another shocker against Manly (38–12), the club was in the process of changing hands. Faced with mounting debt, the Auckland Rugby League wanted to offload its stake in the Warriors. The organisation wasn't in good shape so in came Graham Lowe and Malcolm Boyle, who combined with Tainui to take over the club.

I was just glad the Warriors were still in existence and that I was part of the club. While there had been difficult times I wasn't in any way interested in looking to play my football elsewhere. I was excited to be playing football while living at home around family and friends. I was still a young player in a team full of many more experienced footballers than me, Ali being one of the few who was younger than me when he made his debut that season. So I was content with my lot as a Warrior and it was also a big year personally with Rachelle and me becoming parents for the first time when Chellcey was born on 25 May. That was a story in itself. We played and beat Canberra 25–14 the day before but I had to rush away straight after the match because Rachelle had gone into labour.

Obviously, the season didn't work out well for Frank at all. We'd failed on the field and, with Lowie involved in buying the club, it was fairly clear Frank wasn't going to have much of a future as Warriors coach even though he had more time to run on his contract. With any new owner in an organisation of this type, there'll always be big changes in personnel among management, coaching staff and playing personnel. In this case, Mark Graham was clearly earmarked as the next coach.

On a week-to-week basis in 1998, Frank had been fairly much the same Frank I had always known as coach. There was a strong link between him and Ridgey with Ridgey having a big say on the football side of things. There was great respect between them with Frank being one person — and there weren't many — who could tell Ridgey where to go. It was a relationship that really seemed to work.

Ridgey would still be there for the 1999 season but Frank wouldn't be. I'd be there as well but a lot of that business when Tainui came in was lost on me. That's because, along with Frank and lots of my other team-mates, I was back on duty with the Kiwis once our club season finished, first with the second and third tests of our series against Australia. We began it outstandingly with a 22–16 win at North Harbour Stadium but couldn't claim an elusive series victory when we lost in Brisbane and then back at North Harbour Stadium in the decider. Even then it wasn't all over with 11 Warriors in the Kiwi team that travelled to England to complete a series victory against Great Britain. At least the year had a memorable finale, but more troubles were ahead on the club front.

Marked man

I've been stuck in the middle of a lot of drama during my time with the Warriors and there was always likely to be a recipe for more to come under the Tainui regime. In the end it was a bit like a massive accident just waiting to happen, but it took a while before it reached that point.

Here I was entering my fifth season as a first-grader, not yet with 100 games to my name, and I was already looking at my third different coach, my third different CEO and new owners. That sort of situation can and does create a lot of unease among footballers. When things aren't running quite right they soon sense it and can feel uncomfortable or nervous. That's especially true with matters affecting the football area but management issues also cause anxiety, more so when they affect pay.

I think, though, that I was fairly comfortable with events going on around me by this stage. I'm not saying they went over my head but I was able to live with them, to cope and to keep moving forward. A lot of stuff that went on in the front office we were unfamiliar with yet there were always whispers. I just figured my job was to play football and to enjoy it, which is usually what I tried to do.

The 1998 season had been average on the field and obviously worse off it. The Auckland Rugby League wanted out so new owners came in. If Tainui's money hadn't been available, I suppose we might have been lucky to have a club at all. That kept things in perspective for me because I wanted the Warriors to survive. I didn't fancy the idea of playing anywhere else at that point.

Forgetting the politics, it was going to be difficult for us on the field. Mark Graham had an exceptional record as a player with North Sydney and the Kiwis but he was a new first-grade coach after having some experience as an assistant. The fact he had a seasoned coach like Mike McClennan alongside him had to be a help because Mike, who had good old-style principles about the game, enjoyed much coaching success with Mt Albert and Northcote in Auckland as well as St Helens in England.

There might have been some concerns with our playing roster. With Frank Endacott going, Quentin Pongia departed as well when he signed with the Roosters after only one season in Auckland. Kevin Iro and Tyran Smith also left after stopping off for one year, Kevin heading back to England to join St Helens and Tyran signing for Balmain. Matthew Ridge retired from representative football to dedicate himself to the Warriors and Tea Ropati was forced into retirement.

The biggest setback, though, was losing another original Warrior in Stephen Kearney. He was one player I thought the club should have done everything to keep. He was such a strong influence. He told me he wouldn't be staying and obviously he made a really good move, ending up with the premiership-winning Melbourne team in 1999. Good on him. He was the most professional player I'd had anything to do with and I couldn't think of a person who deserved to win a premiership more but it was an enormous loss for us. He held us together.

Before the 1999 season was out, we also lost Gene Ngamu and Sean Hoppe. Gene was struck down by Compartment Syndrome. No one knew what it was but his calf was tightening up all the time. Of all the guys I played with, he was one of the most talented but he was really unlucky with that injury. He finished in the NRL far too early.

He was only 25 then and headed to England to play for Huddersfield before moving to Australia to play union with Manly. Sean had cause to move on as well, linking up with St Helens.

There was no chance for Mark to splash out big on players. That's the way I understand it and it looked that way with only Jason Death being signed from the Cowboys; he and Mark had a connection through their time in Townsville. The biggest name to join us was Kiwi prop Terry Hermansson, but his arrival came about only through the Adelaide club folding during the off-season. Other than those two, we went into the season building our side around existing talent and by looking to promote some new local faces.

In fact, when you run through the roster, no fewer than nine local products were to make their first-grade debuts that year. Despite that, I think it felt exciting when we started out with new people coming in to take over. We had a new identity and we also had a changed logo with the tongue on the Warrior face being straightened out. We had a new jersey and a new feel in general but there was also some uncertainty with it. There was still pressure on the team after losing quite a few players and after a run of moderate seasons.

In his playing days, Mark had worked very closely with his Otahuhu and New Zealand coach Graham Lowe. Now the relationship had a different look about it. Mark was the coach and Lowie was the chairman. We didn't see Lowie that much. He dealt directly with Mark and Hugh McGahan (football manager) basically.

Of the coaches I've had at the Warriors, Mark was probably the unluckiest of all. I thought he was fairly sound technically. Everyone had this perception of him being a hard bloke — and he was — but he was smart and considerate, too. When they used him in the promotional campaign they pushed the line about all the injuries he'd had and how he played on; in fact, he was actually sympathetic to guys who were injured. He'd listen to medical reports and say: 'If you can play, that's great. If you can't, that's just the way it is.'

Everything he talked about made sense in terms of a game plan but it just didn't work out. He didn't have the strongest squad when you look back over the club's history. Certainly injuries and suspensions didn't help but, as I pointed out, so many players made their NRL debuts that year — Monty Betham, Cliff Beverley, Carl Doherty, Wairangi Koopu, Peter Lewis, Odell Manuel, Francis Meli, Boycie Nelson and Clinton Toopi. That's a lot of new faces when you move forward to 2005, for instance, and note that we had a settled squad and introduced only one new player to the NRL.

But while there was some concern on that front, we started the season brilliantly when we beat the Roosters in Sydney in a Monday night game at the Sydney Football Stadium. While it was four tries each, Ridgey's goal-kicking was priceless with his five from five plus two tries, netting him 18 points. It couldn't have been a better start. Back home to face North Sydney there was a new feel to our match-day operation with no entrance from the tunnel we'd used for the previous four years, no flames, no Pacific Island drummers and no photos or personal songs for each player when the team was announced.

We should have gone back to back that day, playing in front of a big crowd of 20,000. Awen had been on fire against the Roosters and he was again outstanding against the Bears. I suppose he was like Ben Kennedy in a way then. He was at the top of his game, making so much play — but then disaster. He broke his ankle and his season was basically over, although he returned for our last match of the year against Western Suburbs. And on the same day we also lost Monty Betham for the season after he'd made a strong debut off the bench against the Roosters; he needed the first of two knee reconstructions that would disrupt his career. Those were two big injury dents so early in the season, while Ridgey added to our woes with a leg injury and Kiwi hooker Syd Eru's season had been delayed by a wrist problem.

Despite being without those players we had another fantastic outing against Manly in our third match when we blasted the Sea Eagles 36–10. There were signs we were on to something. All too quickly, the wheels fell off, though. The Roosters came to Ericsson to avenge their earlier loss with a 28–14 win and then the season turned completely against Balmain at Leichhardt Oval. Losing the match

17–8 was bad enough but there was much more to it than that. This was the game when Ridgey and Nigel Vagana were both found guilty of contrary conduct over manhandling referee Paul Simpkins and were suspended for three matches each. Tony Tuimavave also copped a three-match ban for a high-tackle charge and debutant Peter Lewis was given a week out on a matter of internal discipline.

The impact of losing the three senior players couldn't have been more immediate and pronounced. When you added Awen, Syd and Monty, we were missing six front-line players and that was never going to be easy to cope with. The list of key players out grew to seven when Doc (Jason Death) had his jaw broken next time out against the Storm — a dreadful 38–10 loss when Wairangi Koopu was thrown in for his debut — and things just got uglier from there on. We were 24–0 down at halftime to the Cowboys at home with the only consolation being the way we kept the score to that in the second half. By then we were forced to play a specialist winger (Sean Hoppe) and a regular back-rower (Tony Tatupu) in the centres.

It was a bit of a nightmare that wouldn't go away as we then lost 12–8 to South Sydney in our next match — when Francis Meli and Clinton Toopi made their debuts — and we just couldn't wait for Ridgey to come back. Even when he did we had another ugly effort when Parramatta beat us 28–6, but he did help us to a fantastic win the following week.

We were 30–18 down to Canberra with just 11 minutes to play when we grabbed two tries, Ridgey converted both to make it 30–30 and then he gave us victory with a last-minute penalty. The trouble was it all came at a huge cost that day because Ridgey got himself in trouble again, and seriously, too. This time he was charged with contrary conduct for running his hand over the face of Raiders winger Lesley Vainikolo, what you call giving him a facial. Lesley really blew up about it on the field, while Ridgey was also charged with a high tackle on Mark McLinden and, all up, finished with an eight-match suspension. That meant we would barely see him all season; in fact, he played in just 10 of our 24 matches and I suppose that probably had something to do with the club coming to an agreement to end his contract. One way or another, he clocked up only 37 games in three seasons. It was a shame because he was a hell of a player when we had him on the field.

With the various defections through injury and suspension, the club moved to find reinforcements. First a hooker was the target to cover for Doc who was out for six weeks with his broken jaw, while Syd's career ended with continued trouble with his wrist. After a search, former Roosters and Bulldogs hooker Robbie Mears was lured from the wilderness that is country footy. That plugged one hole. And when we learned we were going to be without Ridgey for a stretch, the mission was to find a player who could provide some playmaking value as well as being a goalkicker. He was found languishing in reserve grade for Parramatta — John Simon. Initial efforts to secure him for our home match against the Eels were thwarted with Parramatta refusing to release him; instead he was used against us that day from the bench and scored a try in the Eels' 25–18 win. A week later he was playing for us against Penrith. That's the way it goes. John had an immediate and positive effect, though, when we beat the Bulldogs and Balmain before successive losses to Canberra, Brisbane and Cronulla ended our play-off hopes.

The slump through that period when we were without so many players was understandable and it determined the year really, but our run to the end of the season was encouraging when we won five of our last six and each of our last four. One of those was my 100th first-grade match, which turned into a real occasion. Until then we'd never beaten Newcastle but that night at Ericsson absolutely everything worked. Not even Joey Johns could do anything as we blew them away 42–0 — yes, 42–0 — before finishing the year with our highest score in history, a 60–16 win over Western Suburbs. That was the day I scored four tries, equalling the club record, and it all added up to plenty of promise looking ahead to 2000.

One of the great aspects of 1999 had been striking up a lasting friendship with Jason Death. Doc is a very, very funny man, especially with a few drinks in him and he was tremendous to play with. He was a lot like Campo with his attitude on the field, a great buy. He wasn't bad with a fishing rod either.

The biggest positive was being back with the Kiwis for the Tri Nations series, which we kicked off with an amazing 24–22 win over Australia at Ericsson. It set us up perfectly but the following week we had a test scheduled against Tonga at Carlaw Park to keep the team going, rather than sitting around without a match for a week before we played Great Britain. A lot of us hadn't had much football for a few weeks after missing the NRL play-offs so it was understandable the run was organised against Tonga. I know there were thoughts that the match was a waste of time and that there was no way I should have been played in it. Certainly the Warriors weren't pleased but the way I saw it I could just as easily have broken my arm against Australia or in the last match of the Warriors' season, so what's the difference? You're at risk in every match you play. That's the way the game is.

Joe Vagana had smashed into my arm with a shoulder charge when I was making a tackle, breaking my left arm in two places. I needed two rods inserted for the breaks to my ulna and my radius. One pin would poke out if I moved my wrist in a certain direction and the other stuck out around my elbow. It created problems for 2000. I'd been told by the specialist that I should be ready for the start of the new season but it soon became evident that wouldn't be happening. In the end, I wasn't back playing until the eighth match of the season.

Apart from my own situation, the prospects seemed to be brighter for the club. We'd finished 1999 well and, with Ridgey, Sean, Gene and Syd off the books, Mark was in a position where he was able to go to the market for some players. The most notable acquisitions were Ivan Cleary from the Roosters and Mark Tookey from Parramatta, while the club also signed the likes of David Myles, Scott Pethybridge, Matt Spence and Scott Coxon, the last three of whom turned out to be one-season Warriors.

There must have been something of a curse hanging around the club, though, because we again had the cruellest injury luck with key players. After making his club debut, Ivan missed a game through concussion and, in only his fifth appearance, damaged his shoulder scoring a try against Penrith and was out for the season. Tooks also had injury worries which heavily restricted his availability.

This was the year when we also had feeder-club links with Newtown in Sydney's premier league — or Metropolitan Cup as it was called then — plus Souths in the Queensland Cup. While the Bartercard Cup competition was in operation, we had an arrangement that enabled us to fly fringe players across the Tasman to give them some football and we were also able to use some of their players, such as Jason Bell. It was a costly exercise, though, and couldn't be sustained.

As it turned out, nothing at all could be sustained in the end, although we began the year with a great result. In my absence, Mark had decided to run with Robbie at halfback, slotting Doc into hooker for our first match against the defending premiers Melbourne. In the Storm line-up for the first time was my former Warriors team-mate Stephen Kearney. It wasn't a great homecoming for him. We scored three tries to one and won 14–6. The experiment of using Robbie at half was continued for the next two matches but, after they ended in defeat, Ben Lythe was given a shot. Poor bloke. He made his debut against Newcastle and had been going okay as we led 18–12 with a minute to play. Sadly for him and for us he had a kick charged down by Bill Peden who regathered and scored, and Andrew Johns converted to make it 18–18. That was tough.

From there the year went crazy. Tainui, as the majority shareholder, was becoming disgruntled and forced Graham Lowe and Malcolm Boyle out of the club. We went into freefall after that. There was so much coverage in the media about the Warriors having no money and questions being asked about how they were going to pay their players. The CEO Trevor McKewen would be telling us not to worry, that we would be paid this month, just keep coming to training. We had believed Lowie and Malcolm were running things so for them to be sacked was a concern for us as players. You could see on Mark's face that there was so much uncertainty and, in that atmosphere, intensity levels dropped among the players.

On the field, I eventually returned against the Roosters with my left forearm not too bad but not perfect either. I needed massive padding to protect it but I was glad to be able to play again at last. At that stage we'd had only one win — in the first round — in our first seven matches, two of the most recent being a club record 56–12 defeat in Canberra and a 36–8 loss at home to St George Illawarra. The Roosters had so many quality players, not least Brad Fittler and Adrian Lam, but in a thriller we managed to finish in front, 26–22. It was definitely good to be back after a match like that.

We picked up a little with a sequence of a draw against the Bulldogs and wins over North Queensland and Cronulla before we managed another two wins together against the Northern Eagles and the Dogs. That was about as good as it got because in between there was a new record loss — 54–0 to St George Illawarra — and a run at the end of the season that yielded seven successive losses.

It was difficult being at the club then, although I'd seen it happen before so I tended to go with the flow. My job was to play football and I knew if things didn't go well I'd just have to move on. In that climate we had players leaving or talking about leaving. One of them was Nigel Vagana, who signed with the Bulldogs.

We also saw the end of two playing careers and it was sad, I thought, that it had to come about in circumstances where the club was falling apart. I'm talking about Tony Tuimavave and Terry Hermansson. Chief was the ultimate Warrior really, and deserved to reach 100 games. Injuries denied him. And Rock was great value for us in the two years he had with the club. There was certainly a lot of pride and honour playing with both of them and you always knew they would contribute. Thankfully, we were able to send them off with a 32–22 win against the Northern Eagles. Chief had played in the very first match in 1995 while Rock left after topping 150 first-grade matches with South Sydney, the Roosters and us.

It was just an awful year all round, on the field and off it, yet, while it wasn't one I remember that fondly, there was still enjoyment with the blokes along the way. I think that year just proved that if things aren't solid at the top, you'll go a bit sideways and we did in 2000. We've seen the same at other times as well.

I think the fact it was my sixth season and I'd played more than 100 games helped a lot. I was a senior player and I was far more relaxed about being a pro. I'd always taken on a fair amount of responsibility, especially with the position I was playing. I had also learnt a lot by then from the older players I'd been around in the Warriors and the Kiwis, guys like Stephen Kearney, Quentin Pongia, Tony Iro and Jarrod McCracken. When you play with blokes like them you learn that you have to talk a lot to players, being a halfback. I could give it to someone if I had to but most of the time I just kept the guys up and kept them going. I wasn't going to be a shouter.

I didn't count myself as the most professional guy around but I was still happy to give advice if it was wanted by younger players. When I say I wasn't the most professional, I'd do all my training and then my extras but I know I could have been a lot more professional if I'd wanted to be. That I wasn't came down to wanting to have balance in my life as well, to be able to enjoy things rather than building my whole world around football. I'm one who thinks you have to let go sometimes and live life. I don't get carried away and watch every game of football that's on television. I do other things and I also have family as well and they need some time. That's all part of the mix.

Despite what happened in 2000, I still derived enjoyment from playing football. By then I'd had some good years. I thought 1997 was probably my best while 1999 was very good, too, when I managed 15 tries, but there were a couple that didn't work out that well. One of those was 2000 when my arm wasn't right and therefore I wasn't right. Any downside was offset by the brightest news of all when Rachelle gave birth to our second daughter, Waiana, on 28 September. When something like that comes along, footy is suddenly the furthest thing from your mind.

Soon enough it had to come into focus because the Kiwis were headed for the 2000 World Cup in Britain. It should have been exciting but the grim end to the Warriors' year and the near death of the club ensured there'd be some issues to sort out first.

Finals footy at last

L ife as a professional footballer couldn't have been much worse as Tainui's ownership of the Warriors came to an end. Times were really tough then, like nothing I'd been through before and something I don't want to experience again. Somehow the club limped through to the end of the 2000 season but that's all that could be said. We were lucky if we were getting 4000–5000 people to our games, although attendances were officially reported at higher levels than that. That wasn't what worried the players most. We were far more concerned about being paid and, despite assurances to the contrary from management, we kept hearing that we wouldn't be seeing money due to us once our season was over.

While we were paid right up to our last game against Northern Eagles, there was a gap of about two months then until the new contract period started. That meant we were faced with being out of pocket for September and October, which you can imagine we weren't too thrilled about. There were meetings going on all the time attended by the coaching staff and the players as we tried to figure out what we could do, if indeed there was any avenue open to us at all. The Rugby League Players' Association was involved as well — all of this at a time when there wasn't long to go until the 2000 World Cup. Once the club went into liquidation and our contracts became null and void, we had next to nowhere to go. We were effectively out of work, not to mention short-paid.

The atmosphere couldn't have been worse with so many disgruntled coaches, players and other staff. With things looking so bad, I had been talking to Peter Brown about options overseas, most likely in England. But there was also an operation going on to save the club. Eric Watson had come in to take over the Warriors. Well, not so much to take over or buy the club as such but to effectively start it all over again. That meant signing players to new contracts but, because we hadn't been paid out by Tainui, a lot of the guys weren't at all keen. They wanted their old contracts honoured.

Matthew Ridge had played with a lot of us and now Watson had brought him in as an executive director to work on putting a new squad together for 2001. Not long before I was due to fly out to England with the Kiwis, Ridgey made contact at a time when I was also close to sorting out a contract with an English club. He asked me to give him a little time, insisting he'd come back to me with an offer. It was strange dealing with him, as anyone might guess. As recently as 1999 we'd been in the same Warriors side together when he was captain and we'd also been Kiwis together — yet now he was going around trying to sign players up for Eric Watson. Talk about odd. He told me the money wasn't there to pay at the level we'd been used to before. By that, he meant the money wasn't like it had been in the Super League days. That was okay for him. After all, he'd made some decent money out of his career and, as well as that, he'd been paid out of his contract after being released by Tainui following the 1999 NRL season.

The fact I was dealing with Ridgey at all didn't go down well with the other guys. They didn't want me considering anything to do with Watson's organisation. They were telling me not to sign anything because we were out of money after the club had folded. The truth is I needed to sort out my future one way or another. I had a young family, I was about to go to England with the Kiwis and I didn't have a job. I found the squeeze was on me from two sides. Logan Swann and Joe Vagana were heavily involved in trying to extract something after the Warriors had collapsed under Tainui's ownership. They were the two blokes who applied the most heat because they had a belief we should all be sticking together on this, but I believed common sense had to prevail. I know I could have gone to England — and that was a very strong possibility — but my preference was to stay home.

This was where Eric came into the picture. Not for the first time, he'd be involved in keeping me at the Warriors. The key to making it happen in this instance was a meeting Pete and I had at Eric's house in Takapuna. Ridgey was there, too, and it's fair to say it got a bit fiery. Ridgey said there was no ability to give me a contract at the level I'd been on, that the money just wasn't there now. There was some heated discussion about it with Pete holding firm, telling them we had a deal (with Leeds) where the money was way better than what had been offered. Ridgey wasn't budging so Pete asked whether he and I could have a few minutes to talk about things. Pete's view was that we were in a position to sort things out in my favour as long as that was what I wanted. If things didn't work out, he said he would walk out and I should come with him. We went back in and we were just about to go when Eric stopped us and said he and Ridgey needed to talk. The end result was that they came back, the deal was done and I had my wish.

In the end, I was looking at a pay cut to stay, certainly less money than I would have received if I'd gone overseas. That didn't bother me then because I was at the age when football wasn't the only thing. Rachelle and I were happy in Auckland. That seemed to start a bit of a chain reaction with most of the players eventually signing up to remain Warriors. Joe Vagana didn't. He went to Bradford. Robert Mears, Nigel Vagana and Henry Perenara were among the others who didn't stay around, while Logan held out until the last minute before agreeing to terms.

It was just a few days before leaving for the World Cup that I met this guy named Daniel Anderson, our new coach. I'd never heard anything about him before. Most people hadn't. Ridgey had told me he was a young guy with a great brain who had been through all the systems. It sounded exciting to me. Daniel came to the club from Parramatta with recommendations from various places, one of them from Bob Fulton as I remember it. He said we were going to be a young team, starting fresh and my first impressions were good. He told me: 'You're going to be a big part of this. I want you to come back home, have a rest after the World Cup, come back fresh and then start over.' Only three or four players were signed by then but at least twice a week Daniel would be in contact with me during the tournament about players. He'd ask me what I thought of this player or that player and then he'd let me know who had been signed. He and Ridgey were keen on Richie Blackmore, who was then back in England playing for Leeds, so I talked to him a bit trying to encourage him to come back. He was in the World Cup team and had been with the Warriors in 1995 and 1996 so it would be a big plus for us if we could get him.

There were so many other players they were considering. I remember one of them was Jason Temu, a prop who'd had a few games for Newcastle. Ridgey wanted to know about him so I told him Jason was an older guy who had been around for a bit, he was tough and he'd be ideal to have around the club as we went about building a new side. Campo was another one they were dealing with. He'd been signed to play for Warrington and was at the World Cup playing for Ireland, but the Warriors managed to turn that around so he came to us instead.

As the World Cup was in progress, the squad began to take real shape while the front office now had a guy by the name of Mick Watson there as CEO. Of the players that were with the club in 2000, plenty remained such as Ivan Cleary, Henry Fa'afili, David Myles, Francis Meli, Cliff Beverley, Mark Tookey, Jason Death, Jerry Seuseu, Logan Swann, Ali Lauitiiti, Shontayne Hape, Monty Betham, Awen Guttenbeil, Wairangi Koopu, Clinton Toopi and Jonathan Smith. A fair few also went from Mark Graham's side. Terry Hermansson and Tony

Tuimavave had retired while the likes of Scott Coxon, Matt Spence, Scott Pethybridge, Joe Galuvao, Odell Manuel, Robert Mears, Lee Oudenryn, Henry Perenara, John Simon, Joe Vagana, Nigel Vagana and Paul Whatuira decided to move on or weren't retained. Apart from Campo, Richie Blackmore and Jason Temu, the new players in the squad were Richard Villasanti, Justin Morgan, Nathan Wood and Justin Murphy while Motu Tony, Iafeta Paleaaesina and Anthony Seuseu were to make their NRL debuts in the course of the season. The key point was the squad had a share of experience with just about everyone having had at least a taste of first-grade football.

It was still a hell of a mission putting a squad together in so little time and it wasn't made any easier by the fact a lot of us needed a break after the World Cup. That didn't relate just to the boys who were in the Kiwis like Richie, Ali, Logan and me — or Campo with Ireland — but also to those who played for New Zealand Maori or the Pacific Islands teams. That meant the training squad was fairly short on numbers at one point.

With some established players and some younger ones, it was a good way for Daniel to start out because he was a young coach with some new ideas. I remember that off-season we did a bit of conditioning but he had us doing a lot more in the way of skills. What stood out to me immediately was that he was fairly hard on the younger players when working on basic techniques, such as trying to show them how he wanted them to catch the ball and how he expected them to pass it. While he was strict with the younger ones he didn't really try to force it as much with the older guys, possibly because he was so new to the game at this level but also because it was more important to him to have the less-experienced players learning how to do the basics his way from the start. He was fantastic at that, although as a demonstrator he wasn't that great. Well, he was okay but usually he'd get a player like me and say: 'Stacey, go over there and show us how you catch a ball and how you pass it.' Technically he came in and stripped things right back, which was a good thing to do. He was also brilliant showing the older guys a few things.

His ideas on the way he wanted us to play then were fairly straightforward, certainly at the start. Once you were over the halfway line in opposition territory, he wanted his halfback in the middle of the field controlling everything. That meant I had a bigger role coming my way. I was going to do way more than I'd been doing previously when playing for the Warriors. Before, I guess there were other players around me who would have a big say, such as Gene Ngamu, John Simon or Matthew Ridge. They were able to give us a player on either side of the ruck, but that changed for 2001 because Ando wanted the halfback involved in just about everything.

As for the flamboyant style we were known for, he wasn't too concerned. He was prepared to allow that and, within reason, I suppose he encouraged it but his approach to playing the game in that first season was to ensure it was never too complicated. The orders to the dummy half and the halfback were to have a go if you received good ball; if it was on, run it at the opposition.

While Ando was a young coach, it was obvious he really studied the game. He seemed to know everything about every other team, especially their strengths, but he never focused too much on those strengths except with Parramatta. That wasn't so surprising because he'd been at that club and knew their systems and knew their players so well. With opponents, he'd always talk them down and make us feel like we were superior to them. In that way he'd be highlighting and emphasising our positives to ensure the boys went into each game confident; we needed that approach after what we'd gone through in 2000.

All of that was good but we soon picked up one side of him that we had concerns about and that was the way he'd react after a loss or when things weren't going so well. Sometimes, especially when you'd played badly, he'd be so angry and you knew it. You could tell when you saw him the next morning. He wouldn't say hello or acknowledge you at all — but, if it was a win, he'd be your best mate. I don't think that's the right way for a coach to go about it. In my experience, players respond better to a coach who is a little more even in his behaviour no matter what the result, because the way he reacts really rubs off on the players in a big way. We like someone to fairly much be the same person all the time. With Daniel you could tell when he was grumpy. He'd get those watery eyes and you knew exactly what was going on. In his halftime speeches he'd single out some bloke and give it to him. You'd sit back and see the bloke he was dishing it out to and think: 'I don't know whether that's called for.' That's just the way coaches are sometimes and Ando was in that category.

I copped it sometimes, of course I did. By then I'd had John Monie, Frank Endacott and Mark Graham as Warriors coaches and I thought Mark and Daniel were similar when it came to handing out verbal abuse. In saying that, players need to be able to handle it — when it's justified — and just get on with it. For some players a decent bagging helps but for others it actually makes them worse. They're destroyed by it, think about it too much and can't concentrate properly on what they need to be doing. At the Warriors, a coach needs to be careful in this area with a number of Polynesian and Maori boys who might need to be treated a bit differently. I was never a fan of coaches giving players a bollocking and I still have the same attitude about that. Players certainly need criticism and they need to be able to accept it when it's delivered in a constructive way. If you're doing something wrong, you need to be told. That's especially true for newer players but I think guys who have played a fair bit of football already know what they've done wrong and what they need to do; they don't need to be told. To be yelled and screamed at doesn't make it better.

If you're cruising in training or in a game, just sitting back a bit, then you probably need a kick up the arse to get you back on track but, as always, there's a way of doing these things and some coaches have trouble doing it the right way. It's fair to say Ando was the kind of coach who had an ability to go off the deep end a bit too much. He was never a coach you could accuse of being too soft on players. As with so many things in life, there's a fine line between getting it right and getting it wrong but dealing with a group of players at any club, and especially the Warriors, requires a lot of understanding in that regard.

Footballers know their jobs, so at halftime a coach must be able to come into the dressing room and tell them this isn't working so we're going to do this or he has to try to find out from his players what issues they have. Ando would come to me and ask: 'Stace, what's happening? Have you got anything you want to say? What do we need to do?' At least he'd do that the times when he was in a calm mood. I think all coaches are fiery by nature; it's just that some of them keep it in and others let it all out.

That first season with him was one to remember, though. We had some great wins, a share of losses and we played some fantastic football, but above all we made history. The first big achievement was beating Brisbane for the first time. It was a Saturday night match, the scores were locked 12–12 and eight minutes from time I knocked over a field goal for the victory. That match was early on and it gave us so much of a lift knowing we had at last broken through against the Broncos. From there it was a nip-and-tuck process for the first half of the season, the classic case of basically winning one, then losing one. Not until the second half of the programme did we actually have an instance of back-to-back wins — against Canberra and the Northern Eagles — before hitting a patch of just one win and four losses. That's where it could have fallen over but always we had stayed in touch and when we strung together four straight victories against the Bulldogs, Penrith, Cronulla and the Roosters the play-offs were right there for us.

By that time the equation showed just two matches — Melbourne away and North Queensland at home — to go in the regular season and just one win needed, or so we thought. We didn't win either as it happened but it turned out that a 24–24 draw against Melbourne was sufficient, although we didn't realise that at the time. The Storm scored late in the match through Henry Perenara but Matt Geyer missed the conversion. Back in the dressing room, we were all down, filthy because we'd believed we needed to win and, if we'd done that, we'd be in. Eric Watson and the others were in the dressing room jumping up and down and I said: 'We didn't win, we drew.' They told us that was enough, we were in the finals and you should have seen everyone's faces light up. We were entitled to have a few quiets that night because, after seven seasons in the competition and a couple of close calls, we had at last reached the point where we knew we would be playing finals footy. It's the reason why we all play in the NRL. If you can qualify for the last eight, you're in a position where your campaign starts again, where you plot for one win at a time and know a sniff of momentum can so easily take you all the way. Many people would say the Warriors ought to have become a finals club sooner — and we were very close a couple of times — but it was also a reminder of how demanding this competition is.

The outcome in Melbourne meant our next match against the Cowboys at home would be something of a celebration. It should have been. We thought we were going to roll them but maybe we all let our guard down a bit. It was a beautiful, warm afternoon and Ericsson Stadium was jam-packed with a crowd of 24,568, the biggest for a few years. A few of the players let the occasion get to them. I remember Henry, Clinton and Shontayne all turned up with new hairstyles and painted their boots gold especially for the match. Well, Ando knew then that something was up and who could blame him?

The way it unfolded, the Cowboys scored right on halftime through a gift try. Henry had the ball and all he had to do was run out across the sideline. Well, he got tackled and instead of dying with the ball he laid it back for some reason — a brain explosion. The hooter had gone, half the team was walking off and Henry was dancing around, laid the ball back and Robert Relf picked the ball up and ran away for the try. Instead of being just behind we were down 18–6 because of it and, back in the dressing room, Ando just gave it to the blokes with coloured boots. He wasn't big on things like guys who went for hairstyles or did something different, especially if you didn't perform. That was understandable — and that day was one when he and the rest of us had cause to be furious. That's the way Clinton and those guys were. They were young and they wanted to express themselves, although I'd have to ask what goes on when guys do something like that. I'm not completely against it but when blokes do it for match day you can't help wondering whether they have their minds on the job. Are they thinking about the match or are they just thinking about looking good? We played St George Illawarra the next season and there were a couple of guys in front of the mirror putting gel in their hair before the game and Ando erupted. All I could think was: 'Come on, you guys, think about the game, not about your hair.'

With such a big crowd in that day it was a real letdown we blew that match, losing 30–18. Ando had every right to be dirty about it. If we'd won that day we could have finished seventh or even sixth and so missed taking on the minor premiers the Eels. Still, we were in, making it with an absolutely even record of 12 wins, 12 losses and two draws in what was then a 26-match season.

It was so exciting for the club, especially with so little in the way of expectations. No one, not even our supporters, was counting on too much. The only pressure was to avoid the wooden spoon but then the season started taking on some shape, especially after giving St George Illawarra a flogging (34–6), beating Brisbane, drawing with the Bulldogs in an amazing match in Wellington and grabbing two impressive wins against Penrith (52–8) and the Roosters (42–30). We weren't being heavily smashed in our losses either, other than the 48–12 result against Brisbane on the Gold Coast straight after the Anzac Test.

Just making the finals was what mattered most. In 2001 that was the big prize, probably our grand final. That attitude meant our first finals match didn't work out so well. We had lost a few players with injury — Campo and Monty were both out — and the Parramatta Eels were just on fire that day blitzing us 56–12. I don't remember coming up against a more complete team than that Parramatta one, even though they didn't go on to win the comp that year.

Not even a result like that could take away from the year we'd had. It was a major success in a season when everything was new — new owners in Cullen Sports, new CEO in Mick Watson, new coach in Daniel Anderson and a new playing roster. A big part of the success wasn't just Ando but the combination he had with Kempy as his assistant coach. They had a great partnership going until it all went wrong in 2004 — and when it went wrong it went right off the rails. In 2001, they were great, though.

The hot and cold nature of our performances that year was probably typical of the Warriors throughout their history, and something we came to experience again in 2005 when it was just a battle to put wins together. I couldn't quite figure out why that was so in 2001. Maybe it was just that we were so excited, too excited, after a win; we'd have a happy week at training when not too much pressure was put on players and we'd lose the next week. After a loss there was pressure put on players when we were being told we had to do this and we had to do that — and we'd win. We settled into a cycle in effect.

Despite the finish against the Eels we were in a great position for 2002. I was really impressed with what Ando had done for us — we all were. We'd also signed PJ Marsh from Parramatta, which was a major coup, one the Eels weren't too pleased about. Another signing was Brent Webb from the Queensland Cup and Sione Faumuina joined us from Canberra while John Carlaw also came across as a late addition. With Motu and Feka (Paleaaesina) brought in during the 2001 season, the squad was looking better all the time and during 2002 a few more new faces were to come through, most notably Lance Hohaia and Vinnie Anderson plus Webby.

Ando was always of the opinion that you should change things even when they were working well, trying to make them better. That's what probably made him such a good coach — but it was also his downfall in 2004 when we went from being quite an agile team in 2003 that was still fairly fit to a real muscly side in 2004 that was unfit.

But heading into 2002 there was little, if anything, he could do wrong. He had us all fizzing and we didn't just sense we were onto something big, we knew we were. In one season we'd come a long way, turning the club around from total ruin at the end of the 2000 season into a finals club 12 months later.

The holy grail

If making the top eight was our grand final in 2001, it was our minimum goal in 2002. We hadn't suddenly become cocky or anything. We just knew we needed to aim up as we backed up from what we'd achieved the previous season.

We'd gone into the first season under Eric Watson's ownership with a coach and CEO no one had heard of and a playing roster that many people thought had a fair few holes in it. A year later everyone with an interest in sport in New Zealand could identify with Daniel Anderson and Mick Watson and they'd also learned our squad had a fair bit of quality about it. That had only been improved for 2002 with PJ Marsh and John Carlaw coming to Ericsson Stadium as our major signings. Marsh, the Parramatta halfback who could also double at hooker, was one of the most exciting emerging players in the NRL, while Carlaw was a seasoned campaigner who'd made more than 100 appearances for Hunter, Melbourne, Balmain and Wests Tigers. We had the players, we had the coach and, one year on, we also had a club that was well and truly back on its feet after the disasters of 2000.

As for the coach, the more I was around Daniel, the more I realised how one-track his mind was. He was always thinking, thinking about nothing else but football. He was just non-stop. I couldn't have imagined what it was like at home for his wife Natalie; it must have been total football. That's how he was. I guess he would have been in front of a computer screen all the time or watching videos. That's commitment for you, or passion or just plain madness. I couldn't survive like that.

That didn't mean he wasn't able to have a laugh. He could do that. He liked to joke with the guys, punching someone on the arm or something like that and you obviously knew he was happy with you when he was fooling around like that. Something he certainly gave a lot of thought to was our training programmes. That, too, would change each year so, in the off-season leading into our 2002 campaign, Ando looked at a new emphasis. He had us playing a lot of football-specific games at training, not touch as such but games that would get you so tired you had to focus on your ball skills. Another thing he always had us doing was a lot of swimming. I struggled with it, I really did and so did some of the Polynesian boys. You'd see big guys like Tooks (Mark Tookey) and they'd do it so easy. A lot of the others were really good at it, too, and Ando would have us doing it three times a week. On top of that, there was a lot of opposed training, too.

Training was a lot different to what we'd had when Mark Graham was coach in 1999–2000. He used to leave all the conditioning work up to Trevor Clark. We were absolutely flogged back then but there was no enjoyment in the training we did. That wasn't the case with Ando in those initial years. In the summer of 2004–05 our training was similar to what we did in Mark's time, a tough slog all along, although with some variation and a bit of fun to keep us up. That's the way things need to be. I'm convinced off-season programmes should change from year to year. You need a revolving system because I don't think you can keep flogging players. You have to pick your time for that and the 2003–04 off-season was probably one of those times. What we did heading into the 2005 competition was the best thing the coaching staff could have done to us because it was due.

The lead-up to 2002 was my first full off-season for a while because the 2000 World Cup commitments meant I'd had less to do for the 2001 season. I enjoyed it, too. Working throughout the summer gave me a good base and, as well as that, I was injury-free. The only setback for the squad was that PJ injured an ankle along the way so Ando cut back on some of the games and started getting every player strapped before training.

Our overall preparation was still spot-on. We all set ourselves to up our effort levels by 10 per cent; everyone in the club did, including the front office. We all put more in, looking to achieve more again in 2002 with our aim being a home semi-final, the club's first finals match. We spoke about that all year.

As in 2001, we looked at our season and mapped it out into blocks of games. We didn't do that initially in 2001 but once we'd put a few wins together we looked at the matches ahead, sectioning them off into groups of games and setting ourselves a goal of winning say three out of four games here and maybe two out of four there. It was a goal-setting exercise that sat well with the players.

If that was thought out, so was Daniel's approach to trial matches; he'd have a plan for them and he'd stick to it. Maybe it was to start with his top combination but use it for only 20 minutes and then put all the young kids on, changing it around completely. He had his reasons. Looking at combinations was what counted in trials for him and he never cared too much about the result.

With our team settled, we had a good camp at Mt Maunganui just ahead of the NRL season starting. When we arrived, there were some activities on the beach and maybe a bit of gym work on the first day before we were split into groups for the second day. One group would go for a fitness session, do some skills, running and tackling on the beach while the other group would go to the gym. In the afternoon we'd swap around. On the first day we'd all been to the gym, came back, had dinner and Ando said it was fine to have a few drinks because we'd just do some skills the next day. One of the training staff let it drop that Ando was actually going to have a real bash-up session the next morning. He wanted everyone to have a few drinks and then smash us with a tough hit-out the next day. So some of us knew what was going on but half the guys didn't. I know I had a few beers and then stopped but Lance was one of those who didn't. We got back to the hotel and there was a whiteboard showing two lists of players to report at 7 a.m. Basically, the blokes who had kept on drinking were in one team and the next morning they were told to get their runners because they were going to be running to the beach, which was probably about 3.5 km away. I remember seeing Lance and he was spewing his guts out. A lot of the guys in that team were doing it tough. I was just glad I'd had my ear to the ground and knew what was going on.

Before we'd reached that point, there had been one big issue for me and that was the captaincy. In 2001 Campo and I had been used as co-captains and it seemed to work well. I didn't mind the system and I'd really enjoyed leading the side in an official capacity. As we headed into 2002, Mick and Ando said they were looking at changing it, though, and they wanted to have just one captain. They said they didn't know who it would be but it would be a choice between Monty and me. If they were thinking like that I thought straightaway it wouldn't be me who they picked. They asked me whether I wanted the job and I said: 'Bloody oath. I really enjoyed it last year and I want to do it again.'

A little while later Ando called me in to say it was one of the hardest decisions he'd had to make as a coach and one of the hardest he'd ever have to make. He was giving the captaincy to Monty. 'No worries,' I said. 'I'll give him whatever support he needs. In saying that, I'm a bit disappointed but I'll just get on with it.' I saw Monty, congratulated him and told him I'd be there to help as much as I could.

With Monty at the helm, we didn't start our season until the second round after having a bye first-up. It was the Roosters at home and everyone in Australia had been pumping their tyres up after they'd started off with a win. We didn't take any notice of it and worked really hard to come away with a 21–14 victory, a great way to start the season. The following week we were at home again to Newcastle —

and Joey Johns — and Joey had a big day, scoring three tries with the Knights winning 32–14. The loss was bad enough but, even worse, we suffered a huge setback losing Monty for the season with another serious knee injury. As well as that we lost Feka after his spleen was ruptured and Campo had a really bad cut that needed 40 stitches. Back in the dressing room, Daniel was wild, not just because of the loss and the way we played but because of the injuries, Monty's most of all. He abused us for not doing certain things and then, in front of the team, he turned to me and said: 'You wanted the bloody captaincy — now you've got it! Now do it!' He was basically having a go at me for Monty being injured so I just said: 'Sweet, no worries.'

After that, everything seemed to fall into place. We went out and got on the sort of roll all teams love to have at some stage. We blew North Queensland away in Townsville 50–20, dealt to the Northern Eagles 68–10, lost to the Bulldogs 28–20 and then won eight in a row against Melbourne (20–10), Wests Tigers (36–14), South Sydney (25–18), Newcastle (34–12), Melbourne again (28–12), the Sharks (42–20), North Queensland (34–6) and the Rabbitohs again (46–10). The run of eight victories was a club record, the win over the Tigers was a first for the club and it was also the first time we'd beaten the Knights in Newcastle. In that sequence of 11 matches, including the loss to the Bulldogs, we scored more than 400 points and conceded only 160. That was dominance and everyone was taking notice of us. If our attack was great during that period — we scored 20 or more points every time — our defence was even more outstanding.

The Bulldogs game wasn't a great one when we found ourselves 22–2 behind at one stage before coming back to 22–20, but we couldn't hang in there. The one worry for me was that I injured my knee in the 25–18 Souths win and missed the next two matches but I couldn't wait to get back, seeing the way the side was going.

After a loss Daniel wasn't too different to most coaches. Sometimes he'd be obviously disappointed and even angry but other times he was big enough to shake his head and acknowledge the opposition were just better than us that day. You saw the angry side when he believed we hadn't given our best or when opportunities didn't go our way, which was only natural. Again, like a lot of coaches — make that all coaches — he'd have reason to be wild about refereeing decisions from time to time and he let that be known privately at least (but not publicly too much in case a $10,000 fine came his way).

While we couldn't see what Daniel was like in the box during a game, we found out from the reserves just what went on. They'd tell us you wouldn't want to be near him. I've listened to him a couple of times and I don't think he realised the surroundings he was in. He'd be in his own world but that was him. That was the way he coached. He was doing everything the way he thought best, for the good of the team, the good of the club and the good of each player, but it's hard all the same not to take things to heart at times. As players you have to get over it when a coach has a go at you. That's the approach I take. I'd also point out, though, that he calmed down very quickly. Maybe Natalie had a word with him to cool him off a bit. Whatever it was, he wouldn't allow himself to remain grumpy for too long.

I think football was on his mind most after a loss. That wasn't for me. When you lose a game, what else can you do? It's no use thinking about it and thinking about it. That just makes it worse. Other coaches I've had seemed to have some form of release. Take Kempy. He'd go off surfing. And Mark Graham loved playing golf. It's the same with me. I'll go fishing, go out to play some sort of sport — usually with Awen — or muck around with the kids. I was shown by the older players when I first started not to mope around in the hotel room. The best way is to get together as a team, have a couple of beers and get on with things. Sure you could still talk about football but you wouldn't dwell on all the little things. I actually think having a beer after a loss is more important than having one after a win. Not all the time. There are times when you can enjoy a win but other times when you don't want to get too carried away. Again it all comes back to balance and making the right decision in each case.

Of course, there wasn't too much for Daniel or any of us to dwell on during that run of wins in the 2002 season. That's not to say we weren't constantly looking at what we were doing. Daniel kept analysing and we all kept striving to improve. It's much easier to do that when you're winning. The pressures are different. At the same time, there's always the fear lurking that you might slip up. As they say, each win brings you closer to your next loss.

When we did have a defeat, Daniel was the sort of coach who would sound me out as a senior player, letting me know he was looking to put so-and-so into the side this week. What did I think? Or he might say to me: 'You're up against a big forward pack this week but they'll be slow, so you might have a lot of joy.' He turned around and became positive about the next match very quickly.

Another aspect of a coach's operation is the way he goes about naming his side each week. With Kempy, say, he'd have face-to-face meetings with players he was bringing into the side or leaving out. He'd do that before putting the team up on the noticeboard so the players affected knew exactly where they stood. Daniel went about it another way. He'd name his playing side and have six players on the bench but none of the guys on the bench would know who was going to be in, or who was starting. And then it would come to match day and he'd shift players around, moving some back to the bench and others off the bench and into the run-on side.

Probably 15 or 16 players always knew they would be playing but two or three of them couldn't be sure. Sometimes a guy thought he was playing only to find out he wasn't. I don't think that's a great way to go about things. It didn't affect me personally because I always knew I was in the side, but it's not helpful to the team having a few unsure of what is going on, certainly not to the individuals who are affected. I can see the coach would want to keep those two or three players on their toes and it can be worth doing. When you travel and take an 18th man or perhaps two extra players, they'll muck around if they know they're not playing. At training they won't be focused, so then you keep them on edge. The hardest thing about it was the effect it had on a player's friends and family. They're so involved in it and they'd come to a game only to find the player they know wasn't on the field, yet earlier in the week he'd told them he thought he was playing. So you have your mum, dad or whoever asking whether you're playing. You tell them you are, they come to the game to watch you and, hello, you're nowhere to be seen. In that sense, it wasn't good to work like that.

If there was some room for argument there, there wasn't any with Daniel's ability to bring new players into the first-grade side, certainly in the first two seasons. He had some great young talent to call on but he'd be really smart about using it. He wouldn't rush four or five new players into the side; he'd filter just one or two in. We saw that with Motu and Feka in 2001. They came in out of the blue as far as the public was concerned and they were given just a taste of NRL footy at first. It was the same with Webby, Lance and Vinnie in 2002.

Ando also had a good appreciation of club records and achievements. He'd know we hadn't beaten Wests Tigers since the merged side came into the competition; he knew we had never beaten Newcastle at Newcastle; he knew we'd never beaten Brisbane in Brisbane. He made a point of bringing points like that to the team's attention by saying: 'Wouldn't it be great to get over the hurdle and create a first?'

What he didn't do quite so well was his bagging of opposition players. I noticed it. We all did. Whenever he was critical of an opponent, that player always seemed to come out and carve us. Daniel would say: 'So-and-so can't catch the high ball. Kick to him all day. Or that winger there is a spastic. He's soft. He shouldn't be on the field.' So we'd put bombs up and the supposedly weak player would climb up over our guys, or we'd run at the bloke who apparently couldn't hurt on defence and he'd towel us up. We all thought it was funny and used to hope he wouldn't pick on anyone after a while. Whenever it did happen, he'd react the next week by saying: 'I didn't mean you had to lay down the red carpet for him.'

One game he felt uncomfortable about was the home match against Souths when we were up 18–4 at halftime but finished up winning only 25–18 in a bit of a battle. I had to go off that day with a knee injury and Ando wasn't too happy with the way the game played out

Photosport

Open day before the 2001 NRL season finds new coach Daniel Anderson with his co-captains Kevin Campion and me.

Photosport

Campo's right behind me as we lead the team onto Ericsson Stadium for our first match of the 2001 season against Canberra.

Shannon Hegarty rag dolls me after I've scored a try against the Roosters in our 14–8 win at Ericsson Stadium in 2001.

One of my two tries coming up in an amazing comeback win over Penrith in 2001.

Australian hooker Danny Buderus has a hold of me and Bryan Fletcher's coming in to assist in our trans-Tasman test in Wellington in 2001.

We had high hopes for the 2002 NRL season when fans flocked to our open day at Ericsson Stadium.

It looked serious at the time but my knee injury playing against South Sydney in 2002 kept me out for only two games in the end.

In a career that's had plenty of big moments this had to be the biggest when I led the Vodafone Warriors onto Telstra Stadium for our first — and only — grand-final appearance in 2002.

Once the grand final against the Roosters was in gear, a great moment unfolded for me personally as I evaded Adrian Morley . . .

And after getting past a couple of defenders, I slid across for a try I'll always treasure.

Photosport

I went big on the celebrations after my try gave us the lead in the grand final.

Photosport

But in the end there was only desolation. Owner Eric Watson tries to console me after our loss.

Running away from Great Britain standoff Paul Sculthorpe in the third test in England in 2002, the one we lost to square the series.

in the end. The next two matches I was missing so Motu came into the halves; they were difficult fixtures as well, the Knights away one week and Melbourne away the next. I stayed out of things basically as I tried to get my knee right but the boys did brilliantly to pick up wins in both games, especially the one in Newcastle where they blew the Knights away. They were admittedly without their State of Origin players but we'd won a match in Newcastle at last. They were important wins with Ivan captaining the side in my absence.

I came back for the match when we beat the Sharks at Ericsson, although Ivan retained the captaincy. Right through that period, Daniel changed very little. He just stuck with what was working for us then rather than trying to add something new. We relied on our forwards getting quick play-the-balls going forward, we relied heavily on PJ Marsh at dummy half and we also relied on our short kicking game — and, of course, we relied on Ali. Who wouldn't? One of our basic calls was nothing more than 'one up for Ali', which really just meant get the ball to Ali because he could do anything once he had it. Apart from Ali and PJ, Awen and Logan went really well for us in the forwards throughout that winning sequence — and throughout the entire season — as did our props Jerry and Tooks. They were just awesome. In the backline Lance, Toops, John Carlaw, Francis and Henry plus Ivan were all going great and Webby was making a real impact off the bench. The best thing was we had a team with very few injuries and that helped so much.

I think we were able to maintain our winning form through a mix of so many reasons but I'm sure the fact we kept our game simple was the biggest factor. Daniel didn't want to complicate things at all and that helped a lot. The show couldn't have been running better — and then we were hit by a big train smash we didn't see coming. We should have had our eyes open for it but that's the way it works in football. When you're just a bit off your game or your attitude isn't right, someone will grab you in the NRL.

That someone was St George Illawarra on 23 June. Quite why it happened I don't know but it was one of those days when we were just way off the pace. We were without PJ, Wairangi and Jerry for various reasons but were still huge favourites to rack up our ninth straight win. On the other hand, the Dragons were without a lot of their first-choice players with Trent Barrett, Luke Bailey and Jason Ryles all on State of Origin duty while Mark Gasnier, Shaun Timmins and Willie Peters were out injured. Yet the win expected of us never came and it was never remotely possible. They shot out to a 32–8 lead with their young players on fire. Only a late charge ensured the score was respectable at 32–22, but we were really a lot more than 10 points worse than them that day.

Rather than put the skids under us, though, that result strengthened us and maybe woke us up a bit. We proved that when we achieved another breakthrough the very next week by beating the Broncos in Brisbane for the first time, our 26–16 victory at ANZ Stadium coming against a home side recovering from the Origin campaign, although we were also missing Campo, Jerry and Wai. That probably evened things out a bit but we had a magic day, Webby having a blinder off the bench with two tries. The crowd was going off, with so many Kiwis there drowning out the locals when they started chanting 'Warriors, Warriors'. It was fantastic, one of the days I've never forgotten. To beat the team that had been consistently the best in the competition was an enormous accomplishment for us. We'd broken through with a first against them in 2001 at home and now we'd done it away — and there was better still to come.

While there were a couple of losses soon after that to the Sharks and Canberra, our season was made when we accounted for Penrith away (38–24) and then had back-to-back home wins over the Bulldogs (22–14) and Brisbane (18–4). That passage probably took a fair bit out of us, leading to a terrible loss to the Roosters (44–0) — when Ali had his knee injured — followed by another reverse a week later against the Northern Eagles (18–16) but by then we had achieved our aim of a top-four finish and a home semi-final.

By then, too, the season had been turned upside down by the Bulldogs and their salary-cap rorting scandal. They'd been certainties to win the minor premiership until they were docked 37 points by the NRL. It meant the race for the minor premiership had started all over again and we were knocking on the door, although it looked as if Newcastle or Brisbane had the edge.

For our last match Ando decided to rest a lot of us so we could freshen up for the historic home play-off. John Carlaw, PJ, Webby, Campo, Awen, Jerry and Tooks as well as the injured Ali and me were all missing against Wests Tigers but the other boys put it together brilliantly to win 28–12. That was a Friday night match so all we could do was to watch to find out who we'd be playing in the semis. But it turned into something even better. The way the results fell, we were suddenly in with a real show of winning the minor premiership.

What blew us away was the finish in the last match of the final round, Newcastle taking on St George Illawarra and tipped by just about everyone to do what was needed to take the title. If the Knights won or drew, the minor premiership was theirs and they could even afford to lose — as long as the margin wasn't too big — and they'd still be the winners. The Dragons led throughout and when the margin was 26–6, 30–12 and even 30–16, we had our hands on the crown. Then Newcastle scored to cut the margin to 30–22 and the minor premiership looked to be gone — until the Dragons scored twice to take the match 40–22 and give us success through a superior points for and against differential. The unthinkable had happened — the Warriors were the minor premiers and we discovered we'd be playing Canberra in our first home semi-final. With our efforts, Ando was named the Dally M coach of the year and Ali was named the Dally M second-rower of the year but we weren't stopping there. We were after the biggest prize of all — the Holy Grail, the NRL title.

After we lost to the Northern Eagles, Daniel changed tack, telling us he didn't care too much about the game against the Tigers because he was concentrating on the semis instead. He'd given the coaching role to Kempy that week and started making plans for the week leading into our home semi. Now he knew exactly what we were facing, Ando immediately lifted to another level and got everyone around him excited and upbeat about it, telling us how important it was to be playing semi-final football at home and how big an occasion it was going to be.

We knew we were going to beat Canberra in that play-off, simply because we were ready for it. It's my favourite memory of my time with the club, that day — 15 September 2002 — when Ericsson Stadium was a sell-out with 25,800 fans there. I loved everything about that day, the atmosphere the fans generated, the football we played and the result.

We'd prepared for that moment all year really. We'd met our goals and exceeded them by winning the minor premiership but only a win over Canberra would make it worthwhile. In the end victory wasn't a problem as we streaked out to a huge lead before winning 36–20. Ali came on off the bench for his first run since injuring his knee against the Roosters. He'd been on the field only a matter of seconds when I was able to put him into a decent hole to score untouched. It brought the place down.

Walking around the ground afterwards was inspirational. It was so good to see so many happy people in the crowd. They'd been through a lot with us over the years and now you could see the satisfaction they felt.

I suppose we could afford to get caught up in it, too, because we knew we had a week off. As the top qualifiers, success against the Raiders put us straight through to the third week of the finals — only one win away from reaching the grand final. All we could do the following week was take in the action and find out who we'd be up against — would it be Cronulla or St George Illawarra? We also had an interest in the other play-off between the Roosters and Newcastle, with that team going through to face Brisbane.

The Sharks came through on our side of the draw, the Roosters on the other and we knew immediately that we'd be in for a grind in our major semi-final. Against the Raiders, we'd been able to play a freewheeling game but the Sharks relied on their forwards to play the ball for Brett Kimmorley to use. We figured we would have to play a similar game to theirs, aiming to beat them at their own game because we couldn't play loosely and turn over too much ball.

Daniel became a lot more confident and relaxed once we were into the finals. He didn't blow up at all. The way I recall it, we saw a different Ando from the one we had been used to. His halftime talks were calm as he gave us encouragement. I guess because we were playing good football and he'd been involved in winning a minor premiership and being named coach of the year, he felt far more comfortable in his position.

The Cronulla match worked out just as planned. It was tough, a wrestle all the way. The Sharks gifted us our first try when Motu latched onto a loose pass in the first half and, in the second spell, Clinton scored a really classy try when he took David Peachey on and got around him. After a Kimmorley try, it was an absolute grind with the score locked at 10–10. We sweated on an opportunity to break it and avoid extra time and, when it came, it couldn't have felt better — I was able to thread a grubber into the Sharks' in-goal area and John Carlaw timed his run perfectly to grab the try. With Ivan's conversion we were 16–10 ahead with a few minutes to go and it stayed that way. We'd done it. We were in the grand final for the first time — unbelievable.

While we were elated to make it, we had a fairly quiet night in Sydney — but arrived home to pandemonium at Auckland International Airport. The school holidays were on and the arrival area was just choked with kids, parents and all sorts of people. I'd never seen scenes like it. Rugby league had become massive for the entire country now we'd made it to the grand final.

While we were going through Customs, the plan was to stay together. Tooks called us all over to wait, telling us the Customs people wanted to check our boots. So we did, wondering what was going on and then we heard this huge roar: 'Tookey! Tookey!' He'd left us to it and had gone through on his own and got the glory for himself. When you think back to those times even now, it was amazing. People couldn't stop talking about the Warriors. We were all over the front pages of newspapers and there was heaps of coverage on radio and television. The grand final is a major sporting event in this part of the world and this was the chance for the country to discover just what it meant and to really get in behind us.

It also meant the level of intensity picked up. At the start of the season, the first aim was to make the top eight and then to secure a home semi-final. Once we were in the top eight, the goal was to reach the grand final and then to win it. We'd picked them off one by one and now we were left with the last, and most important, goal of them all.

We'd be facing the Roosters, who also had a young coach in Ricky Stuart as well as one of the most influential players in the game, Brad Fittler. They'd put Brisbane out 16–12 and now our focus was on them, on the biggest week of our footballing lives and everything that went with it. No matter how much you try, there's no way grand-final week can ever be treated as just another week. There's too much tied up in it.

We had next to no time at home before we had to leave. After arriving home to the big welcome on Monday afternoon, we had a run on Tuesday and then we flew back to Sydney on Wednesday afternoon. We had to be back there to attend the grand-final breakfast the next morning. Around that we managed a training session at Parramatta after arriving on Wednesday and also had a run on Telstra Stadium on Friday evening. Otherwise, we tried to keep everything as even as we could.

The level of support couldn't be missed. Our team room was overflowing with faxes. There was so much goodwill and the media coverage both at home and in Sydney was at another level. It was so different to see the papers with so much coverage of just one game when during the season there are so many games to focus on. Now the year had come down to the only game that mattered.

The nature of the week made a difference to all of us in some way. Of course it did. Daniel tried to keep things the same but even he went about it a bit differently. On the day of the match, he wanted to talk to every player individually. He hadn't done that before in the previous two seasons. All he said to me was: 'If we win, the player of the day will be one of three players — you, Ali or PJ.' What he was saying was that one of the three of us had to play really well if we were to beat the Roosters.

The bus trip to the ground was different, too. Because we were staying at the Crowne Plaza Coogee Beach, we were in Roosters territory. Around that area and then closer to the ground, there were so many people wearing their team's colours, carrying flags and banners. They were all waving at us and cheering, or jeering at us. On board, Ando had prepared some videotapes to arouse us, footage set to music of all the good things we'd done to be where we were.

Once at Telstra Stadium, the final run-in to the match didn't differ too much from usual apart from the fact we couldn't go out onto the field to warm up. That wasn't permitted and there was no other grassed area around outside the stadium that we could use. That was a bit of a pain because we had to make do with the warm-up room inside, which wasn't ideal.

Throughout this time Ando was just normal Ando to me. Nothing much had changed. There was nothing special about the final message but we were as ready as we could be — and then, at last, it was battle time. Of all the experiences I've had, running onto Telstra Stadium leading the Warriors out will always be unforgettable, one of the most powerful memories I have. To go out onto that ground with so many people there — 80,130 — overwhelms you a bit. I'm not one to get too emotional about things of that type but it moved me that night — 6 October 2002. Now the Warriors were in the big-time. Because we'd made the grand final, there was also an extra formality with not just the Australian national anthem being played but ours, too. That was special and another first, of course.

Bill Harrigan signalled time on and we were into it, my first and only experience of playing in an NRL grand final. We were trailing 6–2 after a really tough first 40 minutes, Ivan kicking a penalty for our only points, although Francis was very close to scoring right on halftime. We felt we were in it and so did Ando.

He tried something different at halftime, though, which I'd almost forgotten about. I guess I didn't take that much notice of it and that's why I've struggled to recall it but some of the other guys did and they weren't too impressed. Daniel put a tape in a machine and played a make-believe commentary of us winning the grand final — the only trouble was the commentary referred to the Broncos as our opponents so that fell flat with some of the guys. I barely noticed it but it probably didn't help. Maybe it wasn't what we needed at halftime. We needed reinforcement and a reminder about areas to pick up on.

Not long into the second 40 minutes, we suddenly had a real sniff when I scored and Ivan converted to give us an 8–6 lead. Everyone says so much about that try, calling it one of the greatest solo tries scored in a grand final. I was just happy to get across to keep us in the contest, but the way I carried on afterwards I guess showed I was fairly pleased about it. After that it was a matter of grinding it out but, as we all know now, the Roosters took over in the final stages and ran us around a bit to win it 30–8. They grew another leg. We started missing too many tackles — 30 all told while the Roosters missed only 15 — and they found quite a few holes. In the end, we just couldn't hold them.

Afterwards Daniel went around the room, shook everyone's hand and thanked them for the season. He was disappointed, as we all were. I was devastated with the result. I'd hoped for and expected a lot better, which made it fairly hard to stay out on the field for the presentations but, with the passing of time, there's one thing that will never change — we made the grand final and we were the first and still the only side to do that in the Warriors' history. We also won the minor premiership, collected all sorts of awards and created a load of records. I never had a year as good as that one with my club.

Finals again, then failure

E ven when times weren't so easy, I'd always been happy to remain a Warrior and stay faithful to the club. Now I felt better about it than ever, knowing we'd been real achievers for two years in a row. This was how I dreamed it would be in the NRL, finding myself part of a team with loads of quality players working with a coach who gave us the confidence to do our job. These were the club's greatest days and they were also my best ones.

As Ando eyed his third year it was fairly easy to work out what ought to be next. Having made the grand final and lost it, the only thing was to make it again but this time win it. To do so, there were a few obstacles, though, and eventually there would be a real roadblock.

One issue concerned me. After the Kiwis' tour to Britain and France in 2002, the New Zealand Rugby League had decided Gary Freeman was no longer the man to continue as coach. The national body had instead shown an interest in Daniel Anderson, which was probably fairly understandable after the job he'd been doing with the Warriors. Ando clearly wanted the post and the club smoothed the way for him to be able to take on the added responsibility.

I had immediate doubts as to whether he should have the position while also running the Warriors. I wasn't sure whether the two would work together so well. No matter how hard anyone tries, I think it has to have an effect when club coaches also have representative commitments. I always wonder how it works out for Ricky Stuart and Michael Hagan, who have had jobs with their clubs — the Roosters and Newcastle — as well as coaching the New South Wales and Queensland State of Origin sides. I can't imagine that's the best arrangement for their clubs.

The other matter that raised some serious questions concerned our squad for the 2003 season. Two of the most important and effective players in our 2001–02 success had obviously been fullback Ivan Cleary and loose forward Kevin Campion. Now they were no longer with the club after being released, Campo signing with North Queensland and Ivan retiring after initially planning to see out his playing career with Huddersfield in England. There were various reasons for losing them, mostly to do with the salary cap I'd say. For one, I know there was a need to upgrade contracts for some of the younger players to keep them at the club; that was fair enough because we had a lot of them who had made a big contribution. While it was good to look after local players, though, it just seemed it was vital to keep Ivan and Campo for another season.

Their looming departure became an issue throughout the end of our campaign and it came up again when Ando and I attended the media conference after the grand final. Asked how he thought we'd go without Ivan and Campo, he said: 'If I've got the guy sitting next to me still playing the way he is and going forward, then we'll be in more games than we'll be out of.' I must say I always thought we'd struggle with leadership through losing those two. We would have Monty back to help with that in 2003 but we still needed another hard man on the field like Campo and we needed Ivan, not just for his goal-kicking, but for his presence, his experience and his ability to play. I talked to both of them about being released but they didn't say too much, just that they were moving on. I guess you could say that's football.

We also lost some others from the 2002 squad such as Justin Morgan, David Myles and Shontayne Hape, but the ones that would be talked about the most were Ivan and Campo. Their names still came up in arguments in 2004, which emphasised just how valuable they had been to the Warriors. While they went, there was nothing in the way of major gains so everything hinged on what we already had in our squad.

The other major negative starting the season surrounded Ali Lauitiiti, who had been sensational for us. Early in the year he needed surgery to remove a cyst from his arm and wouldn't be fit to return to the field until early July. Another player making a late start would be prop Richard Villasanti who'd had off-season knee surgery. Trying to overcome Ali's absence would be quite a challenge.

Also affecting our off-season preparation was the fact so many of us were in the Kiwi team for the end-of-year tour to Britain and France after the grand final. The reward for the success we had was having 11 of us selected for the Kiwis — Francis Meli, Henry Fa'afili, Clinton Toopi, Motu Tony, Lance Hohaia, Jerry Seuseu, Ali Lauitiiti, Awen Guttenbeil, Logan Swann, Monty Betham and me. It was a long tour, too, with a number of other matches besides the tests against Great Britain and France. It was a great honour for me because I had been named as captain but, because we didn't arrive home until early December, I also knew I wouldn't be as well-prepared for the 2003 season as I'd been for 2002. Along with the others, there was no chance to have a smooth off-season; we'd been playing for so long that we needed rest when we returned home so we could freshen up.

While we were on tour, Ando used to stay in touch quite regularly. Because we hadn't really been able to sit down after the grand final, he'd ring me up wanting to talk about that and he also wanted to find out how the tour was going and how the boys were playing so he could figure out what to do with us when we returned. His plan was for us to have skin-fold tests as soon as we arrived home; then we could have a break and come back to training early in the New Year or by about 12 or 13 January at the latest. That sounded good to us.

Daniel also made a point of ringing after the tests to talk about how they went. He said he thought I was playing fantastic football and that I'd had a great year. That was decent of him and I appreciated it. It was during that time that he also told me Monty would have the captaincy in 2003 now he was fit again, which was fine by me. He was the appointed captain in 2002 and I'd supported that choice. It just happened that I had to take over after he was injured. Even when he was out, Monty played the captain's role as much as he could, having a lot to say to us and doing a lot of things with younger guys in the team. He'd also travelled to the grand final with us as 18th man after he'd been cleared from the knee operation that had kept him on the sideline for almost the entire season. No one would have been keener than him to play if the chance arose.

Being away on tour, I obviously didn't have a line on how things were going when the rest of the squad started their off-season training. They had a break after the grand final but clearly the squad was down on numbers when Daniel brought them back together.

While we'd done so much and people on both the inside of the club and outside it must have been looking to us to go one better in 2003, I had the feeling Daniel was actually setting his sights on 2004 as the big one. He knew 2002 had been a long year for us with a lot of us playing a lot of football; I'd played 24 NRL games and then all but one of the Kiwis' nine matches. With that in mind, Daniel probably expected a tired start to the 2003 campaign but would have been looking for us to finish strongly. As it turned out, we started fairly well by winning five in a row after a first-round loss.

As the season started, I was under a bit of heat with a lot of people saying I wasn't playing as well as I had the previous year. I didn't agree. I thought I was going well enough and Daniel told me the same thing. He said everyone was just expecting a lot more from me after the way I'd played in 2002. I'd won the Golden Boot as well so I guess there were even bigger expectations.

I felt I was having a lot of success in the early part of the season, although I guess the fact I wasn't scoring too many tries — only one in our first 11 matches — might have had something to do with the criticism. Ando told me not to listen to what was being said about my form. He said he was more than pleased with me.

Whatever was being said about me, we had a great start to the season. While Newcastle — and Joey Johns — again had our measure with a 36–26 win first-up, we had some decent results after that beating the Bulldogs (24–20), Manly (20–16), South Sydney (38–16), Brisbane (32–12) and North Queensland (30–24), the best of them obviously the one at ANZ Stadium. Yet again we'd beaten the Broncos — that made it three wins in a row against them — and put together one of the best tries ever seen in the NRL; that was the one when Sione Faumuina threw a blind overhead pass for Evarn Tuimavave to score.

Just when it looked as if we were exploding out of the blocks and kicking on from 2002, we started to come unstuck. The first signs were there in the win over the Cowboys when we had a big lead but allowed them to come back at us. If that was a warning, we saw the real impact of it a week later when Penrith beat us, followed by another defeat by the Bulldogs, a win against Parramatta and then two more losses to Canberra and the Panthers again. Ando and Mick Watson were becoming a bit anxious then. We'd gone from a start of five wins and one loss after our first six games to six wins and five losses after 11. It could have turned ugly but Daniel didn't lose focus and held things together fairly well, although soon he had the dual interests of not just the Warriors but also the Kiwis to think about.

In 2003 the annual Anzac Test was scheduled after the State of Origin series so naturally Daniel needed to keep an eye on options for that while also trying to steady the Warriors. And in our next seven matches leading up to the test, we did stop the bleeding by beating Canberra, South Sydney, Manly and the Sharks while losing to only Parramatta and North Queensland. I'd had some joy during that period as well, scoring a couple of tries as well as putting over a field goal for the golden-point win over Souths and knocking over another one-pointer when we beat the Sharks.

The next weekend we had the bye, timed to coincide with a first for Ando — his debut as Kiwi coach. The less said about the test the better. It was awful for everyone involved, a match in which we were savaged 48–6. For Daniel it was a disastrous start to his international career and it also turned out to be a painful one not just emotionally but physically for me.

The test was only 15 minutes or so old when I strained my groin. I immediately knew I was history. I was a liability for the rest of the first half; unable to run, I was missing tackles and I basically couldn't even pass the ball. That's how bad I felt. I saw the doctor at halftime and told him what had happened. Daniel asked the doc for a report and he said I was gone. I'd done my groin and while I had it strapped up I was no better and had to come off in the second half. It was that injury that would severely affect me for the rest of the year and into 2004 as well. While my season wasn't completely over, I was faced with being fairly seriously handicapped in the range of what I'd be able to do once I could play again.

That was to be the only test I played under Daniel and I must say I found him more relaxed in the New Zealand team environment than I did when he was with the Warriors. Maybe it was because there were different players involved, and really experienced ones, too, like Ruben Wiki and Stephen Kearney. He may have been a little in awe of being among players such as them. In many ways it was similar to when he first started with the Warriors in that this was all new to him. He was obviously excited about it but wanted to make it a good relaxed week. None of that mattered after the nature of the performance at Aussie Stadium.

With our NRL campaign reasonably delicately placed, it wasn't a good time to be out of action but I had no choice. I couldn't do anything and had to spend the next five weeks undergoing intensive physiotherapy and recovery work to get myself back into some sort of shape. Lance moved into halfback for the first four games I was out of while Thomas Leuluai played there in the last match. While we were just beaten by Melbourne and also by Newcastle, we put together three vital wins to seal our spot in the play-offs.

The first was a 30–20 victory over St George Illawarra before we went back to back against two of the best sides in the competition, beating Brisbane 22–14 at Ericsson Stadium and the Roosters 26–24 the following week at Aussie Stadium. As contests go, the one against the Broncos was as good as they come, complete with one of the most spectacular brawls the NRL has seen in years. In this day and age I know it's not right to glorify fighting in sport, and you wouldn't find a little bloke like me involved in it, but most people at the ground and watching on television found the brawl that day more than a little exciting, including referee Bill Harrigan. The whole match was riveting with monster hits — like Francis Meli's effort on Brent Tate — and some fantastic attacking football. It set the guys up perfectly for a repeat against the Roosters before I was able to make my return in the final regular season match when we also beat Wests Tigers. I did my groin again that night — even worse this time — and knew the rest of the season would be a huge strain for me.

While we couldn't secure a top-four spot, sixth place was an impressive effort after the flat spots we'd had mid-season and, as everyone always says, it's a fresh start once you're in the play-offs.

That's the way it was for us up against a Bulldogs side everyone had sorted out as favourites to win the competition. They lost that tag fairly quickly after we put together one of the most amazing displays in the club's history. It was freakish being involved that night, mainly because I was in a side in which Francis scored a record five tries himself and we blitzed the Dogs 48–22, an unbelievable score. We did some exceptional things in that match and when I look at the stats now — apart from the nine tries we managed — it's incredible to recall we made 13 line breaks while the Bulldogs managed only seven, just seven errors to the Dogs' 16 and probably the one that really spelt it out, 28 off-loads to a measly nine. Sione and Clinton were responsible for 13 of those between them and they all seemed to stick. To think that could happen in a play-off made the effort all the more astonishing, although, with my groin the way it was, I'd have to say my involvement was limited most of the time. I still couldn't help but enjoy every minute of it.

The contrast from that match to our next play-off a week later couldn't be more acute. Again I needed a load of injections just to make it on the field and really couldn't provide too much for the team. Where we were running free against the Bulldogs, this was a real battle against Canberra. With the scores level at 16–16, we were looking at the possibility of extra time until we worked ourselves into the perfect position for a field goal. While I'd hit a couple of field goals that had been fairly special over the years, none was more important than this one for the obvious reason it put us within one win of back-to-back grand-final appearances.

We'd been fortunate. Throughout the play-offs we were able to field exactly the same combination three weeks running and the benefits were obvious. I was operating well below the level I wanted but we had a great understanding across the park with plenty of strike power out wide — Clinton and Francis were the hottest left-side attack in the competition — and ample strength in our forwards.

Unfortunately, the encounter we needed to win — against Penrith — to make the decider proved to be one match too far I guess. We were in it but the Panthers always seemed to have enough as they won 28–20 and went on to claim the title against the Roosters a week later.

I'd had concerns about Ivan and Campo no longer being at the club when the season started but we made it almost all the way to the grand final without them. Despite losing two of the most influential players the club had ever had, it looked like we were on to something. You had to feel that way after what we'd achieved. We'd also succeeded without going to the market, so that had to be another plus.

If there was some confidence as the season ended, it proved to be misplaced in 2004. I had a terrible off-season trying to get over my injuries, finally having surgery on my groin in December, which meant I'd be pushing it to be ready for the 2004 pre-season trials. In fact, I was no chance at all in the end and, without much in the way of training, I went into the new season well and truly underdone. I wouldn't have been able to be involved because I was either resting or recovering from my injuries, but Daniel obviously got it wrong with our training programme. The senior players realised that, even though the general public wasn't aware of it — and by then it was too late in any case. What happened was that Ando decided we needed a programme that was built around doing more strength work, going for power, and doing very little in the way of aerobic training. It wasn't right and it soon showed. In essence, we weren't fit enough and we weren't agile. All the advantages we'd had in 2002 and 2003 had gone. It was a bad misjudgement and it not only cost us the chance of further success in 2004 but it effectively brought about the end of Daniel's time as Warriors coach.

This all came back to his desire to keep changing things. As I've pointed out, he was always thinking about the game and always trying to find ways he thought would improve us as a team or give us an edge. I think he had targeted 2004 as the big year for achievement and certainly there was a lot of talk around the club about this being our chance to win the grand final. If we'd done things the right way, we certainly should have made the play-offs for the fourth time running, even though we had once again lost a couple of players I would have liked us to keep. One was Logan Swann, who was such a valuable forward for us, and the other was Motu Tony, who could fill a number of roles. Logan had linked up with the Bradford Bulls in England, while Motu signed with Brisbane before finishing up with Castleford and then Hull FC in the English Super League. Maybe there were salary-cap issues again. I don't know. There also seemed to be some differences between Daniel and the two players, which is unfortunate but that can happen. All I know is that we lost two experienced players who provided a lot to the side. The same could be said for John Carlaw, who had also gone after two seasons with us. While they departed, the only signing with a good track record behind him was Tony Martin, who'd been in the centres in Melbourne's grand final-winning team in 1999 and had since been playing for the London Broncos.

The other new faces were former Newcastle forward Matt Jobson and ex-Parramatta back-rower Danny Sullivan, who was trying to make a comeback from serious injury problems.

While our trials didn't offer anything special we still went into the season-opener hopeful of taking something away with us from our trip to Brisbane. We'd won in our previous two visits to ANZ Stadium but this was our first to Suncorp Stadium. We had our opportunities, too, but lost 28–20 and so began a season that certainly wasn't close to one of the best in my time with the Warriors. On a club level it went badly and on a personal level it was really disappointing.

I was struggling through lack of preparation and fitness and, after we had begun with three successive losses to Brisbane, St George Illawarra and Penrith, Daniel was getting really edgy. Success against Manly provided only temporary relief before we slumped again against Newcastle. Serious questions were being asked about the direction we were headed in. This was a club, and basically the same side, that had been in the finals three years running — and in the grand final once — but was now in a fair bit of trouble. Daniel and Kempy were having serious communication problems and Daniel also had words with me about my efforts; I took some of that on board, although there were contributing factors. As I mentioned earlier, it all reached a head when we travelled to Wellington to play the Bulldogs. It was that night that Daniel hooked me from the field and left me on the bench for the last 11 minutes or so of the match. That was his call and I could live with that but what he said to me later that night was something else. With Kempy in the room, Daniel told me I was gutless, that I wasn't showing what I was capable of and that if I didn't pull my finger out he'd drop me back to the domestic Bartercard Cup competition for our next match — but he'd still be picking me for the Anzac Test against the Aussies the next week.

That's when I decided I'd rather stay home with my family than go to Australia. I don't regret that decision and never will. To me, there was no point after that in staying at the club. Retirement was one option, while playing in England was another. Daniel had lost me and he knew that I wanted to leave the club.

At exactly the same time, the Ali Lauitiiti business blew up. Maybe this was a little like my situation. Ando had been obviously frustrated with the way the team was going and had indicated he had some issues with me. It's possible he had the same thoughts about Ali.

The first I knew anything was going on with him was when Mick Watson called Awen, Monty and me into his office after a meeting he'd had with Ali. Mick always liked talking to us about all sorts of issues to do with the team and the club. On this occasion he pulled out a piece of paper. On it were some words Ali had written down — in order, they were family, friends, faith and football. Mick told us this is what you're playing with. I thought: 'Oh yeah, so what?' Mick said Ali was saying he didn't really care about winning a premiership and that he'd have to do something about it.

I didn't think that much about it but next thing I knew we were contacted by phone — especially Monty — to make some comments about Ali's situation. A media release was sent out in which he was reported as saying: 'The players are right behind the management and coaching staff. Players who don't care about winning a premiership have no place at the Warriors. To be a Warrior you have to care about each other and care about the result of the game. You can't stand in the trenches with someone who does not share those aspirations.' The remarks I made were about my relationship with Daniel but it was Monty's comments about Ali that were taken notice of. He was hammered for them. It was unfortunate for Monty but maybe he shouldn't have agreed to have comments like that published.

I spoke to Ali briefly about what had happened but by then it was too late. He was on his way out and off to England to play for Leeds. It happened so quickly and all at a time when I had been talking to Mick about leaving as well. With Ali, I still don't get it. So, he was one of the higher-paid players and he had some form problems but he was in exactly the same position as me. He'd had surgery on his arm and was struggling for fitness and form when he came back but the club ended up not sticking with him. I think more loyalty should have been shown to Ali. He wasn't fit enough or where he wanted to be at that time but, with a bit of patience, who's to say he wouldn't have rediscovered his form? After all, he has done really well for Leeds. Clearly, Ali had needed a different training programme in the off-season leading into the 2004 competition. Of all the players in the squad, he was the one who needed lots of aerobic work rather than concentrating on power, but that was Ando's call so I suppose Ali was a victim of it in the end.

The loss to the Bulldogs proved to be Ali's last outing for the club and Daniel was also well aware of my plans then. It made life difficult at the club, Ando reacting by switching me to standoff as he considered who to develop as my long-term replacement. I understood the need to do that and kept contributing as best I could.

We actually rebounded from Ali's departure and my issues in Wellington to beat Melbourne 20–14 in our next outing but were beaten 16–8 by North Queensland in a dreadful match. It was my 200th first-grade appearance, which should have been a cause to celebrate but both sides were awful that night; we just happened to be even worse than the Cowboys, which was saying something. For all that, we seemed to slip even further when we were back home for Manly the following week. I had some personal satisfaction scoring two tries but, after leading, we just caved in, allowing the Sea Eagles to win 42–20.

Ando was well past making excuses by then and gave us a real spray at the media conference when he said: 'It was embarrassing. I thought we rolled over. Personally, it's a slight on my character as a coach and our character as a team. I feel let down. For them to go through us means no one gives a rat's arse about the blokes next to them. They're all worried about themselves only.' And Mick spoke in much the same vein when he said: 'It's almost like I feel an apology is required to the fans and people who've sat in the rain since 1995. We promised we wouldn't be the old Warriors but after today we are.'

It was difficult to argue with what they were saying because we just weren't cutting it. I felt sorry for the fans, too. I'd have to say, though, that we were trying. We never went on the field and gave in, which Ando thought about our effort against Manly. I wouldn't accept that. Then again, I couldn't make excuses for the way we were playing either. Instead there were two facts: we were down on confidence and we weren't fit and so much of that came back to the way we'd prepared for the season.

We didn't know it then but Daniel didn't have long to go in the job. After managing just our third win in 10 games — beating South Sydney 26–12 at Aussie Stadium — we were back at the same ground to play the Roosters a week later. By the end of that game, we were lucky to have avoided a record defeat as the Roosters towelled us up 58–6. It was just the worst display out and Daniel made sure we knew it. Early the next week, we met in the team room and he made us watch the whole match. He put the tape on, told us not to turn the volume down or fast forward it, to watch and listen — and then he walked out of the room. It was the last time he would speak to the team.

When we arrived at the club on Thursday we knew something was going on and soon enough we figured out what it was. We had been guessing as much during that week and it wasn't any great surprise when we were officially told Daniel had gone. Eric Watson was home at the time and he had a few words to the players. They were tough times for the club but, despite Daniel going, my mind hadn't changed about leaving at the end of the year. I was still committed to that thought at the time.

It didn't add up to me that Ali had left. That was a shock. I can't say the same about seeing Daniel go in the end. It had probably been building the way things had been going but that night I rang him to wish him all the best. Like a lot of the boys, I owed him plenty as a coach. He'd done so much for the club in his first three years and a lot for me, especially in his first two years. It looked like he had the Warriors heading the right way and could have been in the job for as long as he wanted — but all too quickly things started going wrong. Maybe some cracks were beginning to appear in 2003. Whenever they started, it was still difficult to believe he could be so assured in the role for three years but then lose it. We'd gone from grand-final hopefuls starting the season to wooden-spoon contenders inside three months. It was no easy time for a new coach to come in but someone had to do the job.

Come in, Kempy

It was like a recurring dream. In 1997, John Monie's coaching career with the Warriors came to an abrupt end after a poor run of form in Super League's Telstra Cup. The board said enough when a loss to North Queensland — our third on end — left us with a three wins-six losses record after the first nine matches of the season. John was there one day, gone the next and hardly heard of for days. So in came Monie's reserve-grade coach Frank Endacott at the worst time imaginable. It had to be a poisoned chalice taking on the job and, despite his best efforts, his time as an NRL coach lasted just a season and a half.

Now fast forward to 2004 and I was seeing it happen all over again. After half a season of discontent — three wins and eight losses in 11 starts — we watched as Daniel Anderson disappeared from Ericsson Stadium. And there to pick up from where he left off was his assistant coach of three and a half years, Tony Kemp. Just like Frank, it was a mission just to see through the rest of the year and then try to start off fresh for the full season to follow. Sadly for Kempy, the story would have the same ending because he, too, had no more than a season and a half in the top job.

When he took it on after Daniel's departure, I was pleased for Kempy despite it being a difficult time to step up. He had a mission in front of him but I wanted to believe it would work out. I'd known him for a long time, playing with him when I first made the Kiwis for the 1995 World Cup in Britain. He was 27 then and I was only 19 when I made my debut against Tonga at halfback, while he was at loose forward. We were team-mates again for our other two matches at the tournament. Kempy and I had actually come across each other as opponents in the Winfield Cup earlier that year when I was playing for the Warriors against his South Queensland side. His international career finished after the World Cup but five years later we were in the same set-up again, only this time as player and assistant coach.

He didn't hesitate to put up his hand to replace Daniel at the Warriors, even though the job was his only on a temporary basis at first. He told me if he was given the job long-term he really wanted me to stay, to go back on my decision to leave at the end of the year. I got on well with Kempy and the way he felt about things was a factor when I finally decided to stay. I'd found him a very good coach when he was assistant and I thought he'd do a decent job as head coach.

There'd been some stupid stuff going on between Daniel and Kempy that year when they weren't talking to each other. It was shocking for the players to see that but we had no idea what had actually gone on between them. We had the head coach saying one thing to us, the assistant saying another and the two of them not talking to each other; it wasn't good but with Ando going that wasn't a problem now. That, too, had been another piece in the puzzle that had added up to my decision to go in the first place.

Through that period Daniel had been playing me at standoff and obviously that was being done to look at options for the following year. While I could see why that was being done it further fuelled my wish to leave, or to stop playing. I was in my 10th season with the club and I began to ask myself whether I had the desire to keep playing. In fact, I told Ando when he came back from the Anzac Test that I was going to hang up my boots. He had called me into his office, shown me a list of players the club was trying to sign and asked whether that would make me feel any better about things. I told him it didn't, that I was just over it with everything going on.

Kempy stepped in with a just a few days to prepare for our home match against Canberra on 6 June. The side had been named by Daniel before he left so I was still listed to wear the No 6 jersey but, once Kempy had the job, he told me he'd shift me straight back to halfback.

That game was played on so much emotion, probably too much looking at what happened with the judiciary afterwards. Under NRL rules I was meant to wear the jersey number I'd been originally named in — No 6 — but Kempy told me to put on my favoured No 7 with Lance Hohaia putting No 6 on. That carried a potential fine but it was important psychologically to make the change, to go back to the way we used to do things. It was a great day for the club actually, a real positive after what had been happening and we came out of it with a 20–14 win, but the emotion of the day caught up with us. Jerry Seuseu was pulled up on a few things and was given a seven-game suspension (and he'd only just returned from a one-match ban). As well as that, Francis Meli was suspended for five matches and Sione Faumuina for four. So in one swoop we had three of our most important players sidelined for a total of 16 games. We were low on numbers as it was, so to lose them wasn't good at all for us.

The whole coaching situation was awkward for Kempy. Coming halfway through the season, there was no way really that he could change things around too much. He had to stick fairly much to what we were doing but he wanted to get the boys back to trying to enjoy their footy. He tried to keep us all upbeat, saying he didn't know about his future at the club so he was just treating it as a week-to-week experience at first.

It was an unsettled time to say the least as it became clear quite a few players would be leaving, including Henry Fa'afili, Mark Tookey and Justin Murphy plus two of the 2004 signings, Danny Sullivan and Matt Jobson. Later on PJ Marsh was released as well and so was

Thomas Leuluai, while Ali had gone quite a bit earlier. PJ's loss was a huge one. I played my best football when he was in the side. He was so dynamic around dummy half and took a lot of pressure away from me. His injury was terrible — a bulging disc in his neck — and he needed two operations to fix it. He was unable to play football for 18 months and you could see the club's position to a certain extent but, when you saw what he did in 2005 when he was back with Parramatta, it probably didn't look like a good decision to let him go. It was a long time out of football and, at the same time, Ruben Wiki and Steve Price were players on the market who we really needed. If the club had taken a risk on retaining PJ they wouldn't have been able to get Rubes and Pricey or Nathan Fien.

On the positive side, we were encouraged when Fieny signed from the Cowboys and a few weeks later the big ones — Ruben and Steve — were announced. Signing them was a brilliant effort after some great work by CEO Mick Watson and our general manager Spiro Tsiros. We were all pumped when we found out they were coming.

As for the rest of the 2004 season, moving on would be the best thing to do. Of the 13 matches under Kempy, we had some shocking losses against Wests Tigers — straight after the Canberra win — Melbourne, Parramatta and the Bulldogs but we were also desperately unlucky to lose tight ones to North Queensland (28–26) and Canberra (30–29). After the Raiders, there were just two more wins against Parramatta and South Sydney as we finished equal last with the Rabbitohs but escaped the wooden spoon through a superior points for and against margin. We were the worst attacking side, scoring only 427 points and the 693 points ranked us the third-worst defensive side in the competition.

Like everyone else connected with the team and the club, I felt it was a relief when the season was over. Kempy had been confirmed in the head coach's job by then — which was the least he deserved — and there'd been more positive news with my former team-mates Ivan Cleary and Kevin Campion coming back to Auckland to join the coaching team. Awen Guttenbeil, Monty and me had been kept in the loop when Mick was looking for an assistant coach and Ivan and Campo were mentioned along with a few others. Their names stuck out to us and so they came on board. It was exciting for me because, of the four on the coaching staff, I'd played with Kempy and Tony Iro in the Kiwis and with Ivan and Campo when they were first at the Warriors. As well as that, former Roosters winger Todd Byrne was later added to the playing squad so there was every reason to look forward to the off-season.

We'd always had a lot of trouble with players leaving the Warriors, though, and just before the season there was another one when we lost Vinnie Anderson. I don't know what went on there but we could have done with him. I know he had been given medical advice not to tour with the 2004 Kiwis, so he could rest a chronic injury he had in the pubic area, but this is where it's club against country and this is where the game is in a real mess. Guys really want to play for their country but the clubs want them fit and well to start the next season and that's where it's such a tough position for everyone involved. We've seen it at Penrith with Tony Puletua and Joe Galuvao, at the Bulldogs with Sonny Bill Williams and Matt Utai and Wests Tigers were making things difficult for Benji Marshall in 2005 as well. Then there was a guy like Vinnie. He had the chance to tour somewhere he hadn't been before, he loves playing for his country but he had an injury that needed rest. Before the tour our players were told they'd have to be straight back into training when they returned home. I think a few of the boys weren't happy about that; I wouldn't be either but they were told before the tour and they all agreed to it so they should have been able to go along with it. We knew we had to work so hard in the off-season after the events of 2004. That had to happen no matter who you were.

As for the 2005 season itself, it had a lot of very good moments but also too many that were, well, disappointing. There was no other word for it. In my whole career I'd never had a year where we had so many close defeats and so many matches where we were in them virtually all the way. Actually, there wasn't a match that we didn't have some sort of chance of winning; we were never pounded while opposition teams managed to top 30 points only four times, Penrith (42) putting the most on us. It was so much better than 2004.

I had added responsibility as the first-choice goalkicker, a duty I took very seriously and worked on as hard as I could. While my kicking could have been a little better — I managed a 70 per cent success rate — I don't think we lost games through missed opportunities. In fact, we won games through it such as the 24–22 win over the Roosters, the 24–16 victory against Canberra and the last match of the year when we beat Manly 22–20.

But what really stood out was the on-off nature of our season from the outset. We were dirty on ourselves for not starting with a win against Manly but atoned for that with a great win over Brisbane, our first at Suncorp Stadium and our sixth in our last nine encounters with the Broncos. It should have set us up for the Cowboys at home but we slipped up there, beat South Sydney, lost to Wests Tigers and then came back from nowhere to beat the Knights in Newcastle. We just never settled into the sort of rhythm we'd hoped for.

Towards the end of that sequence of six matches I was also having an awkward time personally in the weeks and days leading up to my decision to go to France. I felt so many pressures from all sorts of places. I was talking to UTC but I was in no position to say anything until the deal had been done. You don't talk about your negotiations publicly; you go through a process and, once I had committed and had everything sorted out, then I was able to confirm what had gone on — but not until then.

It irritated me having so many people demanding to know when it was none of their business. It's a stressful business going through negotiations like that and this was an important step for Rachelle, our girls and me. We were going to do something totally different after all those years with the Warriors and living in Auckland. Once I'd announced my decision, though, so much pressure was lifted off me and I started enjoying going to training, playing and everything about my football. It became a bit of a celebration knowing I was counting down to my last days as a Warrior.

I remember after my last home game against Newcastle, Kempy told the media I'd paid him the ultimate compliment by saying the 2005 season had been the most enjoyable in my 11 years as a Warrior. A lot of people wondered about that. How could you enjoy a year when you didn't make the finals? What I actually said was that it was *one of my most enjoyable* and that's true. It was. I'd had such a good time with the boys, I really looked forward to training and wanted to do everything I could to make my last season a memorable one. There's no way I was going to wind the clock down and just look forward to it all finishing. From the moment I started, I had a fantastic time at the club and loved the place so much but I was also so excited about what I was going to be doing in 2006.

Of course, the results weren't so exciting in 2005, especially when we went through a sequence where we lost by two to Penrith (16–14), four to Cronulla (28–24) and four again to the Roosters (10–6). They were heart breaking, especially the first two when we were leading but lost both times by conceding late tries.

I had special reason not to forget the Cronulla match in Perth. The longest trip in the NRL and I went all the way there and didn't play! I wasn't too happy. I had a hamstring strain I picked up against Penrith and I thought I probably could have got through the match but the decision was made for me and it was probably the right one. I was just angry I had to go all the way over there when I could have stayed at home and done my rehab there. It was quite funny, though. Kempy knew I wasn't happy and I was flogged at training every day and when the boys played it was my birthday that day. I was blowing up. I'd been told I'd have to train the day after the match as well — we were going home on a later flight — and we went out for a few drinks. Awen and Kempy told me: 'No, you don't have to train tomorrow.' And they kept feeding me more beers. Then the next morning Kenny Reinsfield got me in the boxing ring and flogged me — and I threw up. The guys had done the dirty on me.

From having only three wins from our first nine games, there were better times when we twice put together back-to-back wins (Souths and Wests Tigers and then the Roosters and Canberra), which hadn't been done since 2003. Outside that there were only three other victories, the 30–18 result against Brisbane in our 10th anniversary match — a great day and a fantastic win — plus a home win against Melbourne and our final effort over Manly. The way the competition worked out, we were still a top-eight possibility right down until our second-to-last match of the season and my home farewell against Newcastle. The close defeats kept coming in what was a very even season with a five win-seven loss record both home and away — but 10 wins wasn't going to be enough to make the top eight and we had to settle for 11th, only four points off eighth spot.

The season was definitely disappointing personally and from a team viewpoint. In saying that I came to training and came to play to enjoy myself, which I think I did. I said to myself that nothing was going to get me down and that helped me a lot. We made a lot of inroads, although there are obviously areas we need to change.

If I was to break it down, one of our worst areas was still discipline. We might perceive ourselves as being targets for the Australian referees but whether that's true or not, discipline has to be a big part of our game and it still needs a lot of improvement. The team's error rate was a problem — like dropping the ball, running the ball over the sideline on tackle two and things like that. It just showed we had no brains, no smarts. That applied across the team. I believe the major issue is that we're a team that doesn't understand football. We suffer through too many players who show a lack of understanding at crucial times in a game. It might be the 23rd minute of a match when all we need to do is to complete a set and someone throws a pass out the back on an early tackle. Why? Because they don't understand how important it is for us to complete that set. To me that's all that needs to be taken care of to make this a very successful team.

Too many of our players still haven't learnt to be mentally tough. Actually, it's not that. It comes back to what I said first — they need to understand the game and why you do certain things at certain times in a match and why you don't do them at other times. Brain explosions — that's what we're talking about. In terms of strength, size, speed and skills we don't have anything to be worried about and we also made big improvements defensively until we fell away a few times at the back end of the season. Then it was a matter of missing too many one-on-one tackles.

Our attack was slow at the start of the season before it came good later on but, whenever you play under a new system as we were in 2005, the attack is the one area that takes more time to get used to. We had difficulties with Daniel's system in 2001 but in 2002 and 2003 it took care of itself. I think the system brought in under Kempy was definitely right, but there were little areas that needed to be fixed up and that's up to the individual.

A lot of responsibility rests with each player but it's up to the coach to ensure the week is running smoothly so preparation is spot on. There were times when our preparation wasn't right. One example was after we'd beaten Wests Tigers 21–4 at Ericsson. We'd played well, the boys were all in a good mood and that night Lance went out and got himself into a bit of trouble. The next day we're called in for training and the coach isn't talking. He's fuming and we don't know what's going on. Kempy came in and told us one of our team-mates (Lance) had shat on us and he was going to take it out on all of us, not just Lance. So we were taken out onto the field and had the shit flogged out of us. We just thought that was bullshit. We'd busted our arses the day before, won the game and this was how we got treated. It was too heavy and we went from feeling good about ourselves to feeling down. It upset our preparation, as we saw that week when we played like pansies against St George Illawarra.

That was a consequence of what we'd agreed to at the start of the season. It was all about collective responsibility, which meant the whole team gets punished when something goes wrong. That was one side of it but I know Ivan and Campo, who took that penalty session, weren't too happy about doing it. I accept discipline had to be sorted out this year and the club has come a long way with the things Kempy brought in and put in place. It had got a bit out of control with guys turning up late all the time. That was tidied up but, as with anything, there needed to be a balance and with that instance they went too far the other way.

It wasn't just preparation that was a factor the week of the St George Illawarra match. There was also a question for me about the captaincy again. When Pricey had been out of the side on Origin duty for the Souths match at North Sydney Oval, I'd been given the captaincy and I took over again when he left the field with his injured knee against Wests Tigers. Throughout that time Monty, who was the appointed vice-captain, had been out suspended for six matches and then he came straight back into the side as captain for the match against the Dragons. Kempy didn't say anything to me about it. Monty was simply named as captain in the team posted on our noticeboard. I saw it and took a bit of a step back in terms of leadership for the match in Wollongong, allowing Monty to lead the side.

After the game, Kempy asked me why I wasn't being the leader. 'Because I'm not the leader,' I told him. 'That's Monty's job.' I think the coaching staff had a bit of a talk about it and decided to give me the captaincy for the time Pricey was out. Monty was a bit funny about that then. It was like when the captaincy was taken off me the first time after 2001. Being the captain means a lot to me. I'll always be a leader as a senior player on the field and in the position I play but when you're captain, you're at another level. You have the final say on everything.

Obviously, the real focus eventually went on our failure to make the top eight. It was all very well to say we had improved on last year, but was it enough? That was the question asked over and over. Before the season finished, we started to see the signs of big change at the Warriors. Already some players who had been with the club for a long time were going; apart from me, Francis Meli and Iafeta Paleaaesina were on their way and in the days after beating Manly it was confirmed Monty Betham had asked for a release. The big news, though, was Mick Watson's decision to leave after five years as CEO, which was announced the week we travelled to Sydney for my very

Mud, glorious mud — I don't think so. The infamous mud run was part of our off-season preparations for the 2003 season.

The best player I came up against was undoubtedly this man — Newcastle's Joey Johns. He had it over us again at Ericsson Stadium in 2003.

There's a fair chance I'm celebrating a win — and I am. This is after slotting a field goal for our golden-point win over South Sydney in 2003.

There were just a few good times in 2004, this being one of them when captain Monty Betham and I walked off Ericsson Stadium after we'd beaten Canberra.

Of my 11 seasons with the Warriors, 2004 was the most challenging, especially on this day when we were mauled 50–4 by Wests Tigers in Christchurch.

A new season and a new attitude . . . coach Tony Kemp and I wind down after another off-season training session.

This was one to remember, the whole crew lapping up a great 30–18 win over Brisbane to mark the 10th anniversary of the Warriors' first match.

It's all over now and Waiana is there beside me as the boys give me a guard of honour after my last home match for the Warriors. Sadly, it was a losing farewell against Newcastle.

All alone in the locker room — my Nikes are off and the strapping is coming off, too, before I head to my farewell party.

A week later it was goodbye again, this time after my last match in the NRL, a win against Manly in Sydney.

No, it's not me in Lance Armstrong's cycling colours. It's the strip I'll be wearing for my new club UTC — or Les Catalans — in the English Super League in 2006.

last NRL match against Manly. It was a bit of a shock when we all met in the team room to hear Maurice Kidd, the Cullen Sports chairman, tell us what was going on. Mick was there and he spoke to all of us as well.

I think it was the right thing for both the club and for Mick. He'd been there to build the club up after it had been a basket case in 2000. With all the success we had in the first three years, he tried to make the organisation a bigger concern and that came back to bite him basically, especially when he tried to move into rugby union. He also brought in the boxing business with Shane Cameron, Danny Codling and Kenny Reinsfield. I thought that was fine. It was good having them involved. Shane was a great bloke to have around the club, proving an inspiration to a lot of us. I would have kept the boxing guys involved inside the club but the board has gone the other way.

When Mick was working on other projects like the rugby union one and the boxing, Daniel had complete control of the football side, but then things started to go wrong in 2004 and Mick had to come back into football to try to fix it up. I know when Eric took the club over and Mick was brought in as CEO, he and Daniel lived and breathed football. They had to go like crazy to sign players so we had a team for 2001 and they talked a lot about what they had to do but, in time, Mick wanted to look for other challenges so he headed off into other areas. When he was involved in football, he obviously knew his stuff. In my time with the Warriors, I had four CEOs and Mick was by far the most involved in football. He had me and other players in his office all the time. He was always asking me about other people, the coaches and players as well as wanting to know how I was getting on. It was good because he was interested. At the same time, I knew he was trying to put some thoughts in my head but it was his way of keeping in touch with what was going on. I was careful about what I would say, even though I knew he was doing it for the benefit of the club. Sometimes it didn't sit well with me, like the business about Ali Lauitiiti and his departure.

As a CEO, he did some really good things and some not so good things. It's just like football. As players we can't do it right all the time. Mick put a hell of a lot into the job, though, and brought the club back to life. He put himself out there and copped a bit of flak but he knew that would happen. On the football side, I would have preferred it if he hadn't been as involved as he was but I also know he felt he had to do it. He's a bloke who knows the game. He played it to a reasonable level and that encouraged him to have his say. Remember, too, his job was on the line so he had to feel as if he was doing what was best for the club. Whether that was the right thing to do is the question. He obviously felt it was.

There were some younger players who didn't like Mick but he also had staunch supporters like Monty and Awen. Mick came on board while I was away at the World Cup in 2000. I spoke to him on the phone and, when I came back, I soon saw how much energy he had. When he spoke to you, he really got you up. There was one thing I wasn't so sure about and that was the way the New Zealand Warriors, as the club was now known, cut themselves off completely from what had happened with the Warriors before they arrived. Along with Awen, Monty and others I was part of the club's early years and there were plenty of times I enjoyed along the way. I wasn't starting clean as a new Warrior in 2001; I was already a Warrior. I think the club's history is important and it's great when we celebrate something like our 10th anniversary as we did against Brisbane in 2005.

Mick put some good plans and systems in place. We used to have a conference a week before the first competition game. When we first did it, Eric spoke to us and that was really good. The season would be mapped out with estimates on how many wins we had to get from small blocks of games and we went away with a focus. In the first year, Eric came to just about every game we played and he spoke to us when we first made the play-offs. We loved having him involved, seeing the owner there and showing so much interest. He would be around us when we won and he'd be there when we lost to pat us on the back.

Mick's era ended after two years that weren't anywhere near as good as his first three, his resignation signalling the club was clearly moving in a new direction — and there was more to come. There had been plenty of speculation about Kempy's position as well and now it began to intensify. That became a focus of an end-of-season review conducted by Cullen Sports chairman Maurice Kidd and John Hart. I thought the review was important but, with the season not running the way everyone had wanted, I think it's easy with a process like that to push the blame onto someone else rather than yourself. I hope the other players involved didn't go in there and just heap the blame on Kempy. That wouldn't have been fair at all because players always have to look at themselves as well.

I hope Maurice and John didn't look at the review as a way of ganging up on one person. I was one of the players involved in the review and I was asked what I thought of Kempy, Ivan and Campo plus some other questions. I guess other players interviewed were asked the same things. About a week later, Kempy was out of the job when the club announced the new coaching structure with Ivan as the head coach, John Ackland as assistant coach, Campo as skills coach and Tony Iro as development coach. Keir Hansen was still there as head conditioner, Don Mann was the new football manager and John Mayhew had come in as medical director after Chris Hanna finished up in the position. When I heard about it, I thought Kempy might have been a bit hard done by considering where we had been in 2004 and where we finished in 2005. We'd made progress and had just missed out on the play-offs. There's such a fine line between making the finals and missing them. Make them and it's viewed as a success, miss them and it's regarded as a huge failure no matter how close you are.

I thought it was fine using Maurice and John to do the review. It was a bit difficult for them because Mick had resigned as CEO. He had some involvement in part of the review but not the interviews with the players, where normally the CEO would have been heavily involved in an operation like this. With John and Maurice running things, there was no one with a real league background but they also spoke to people outside the club to balance that. This is not the place for me to repeat what I told Maurice and John. That wouldn't be right but, if I was still around at the club, I would have been happy with either Kempy or Ivan as head coach.

I must say I didn't think the coaching structure worked this year, having Kempy as head coach while Ivan was the offence coach and Campo the defence coach. What happened was that Kempy would tell you to do something but Ivan and Campo would tell you something else again. They didn't seem to know what they were all saying. Maybe there was a communication breakdown. I know Ivan wanted to become a head coach sometime and, when results weren't going his way, I'm sure Kempy was looking over his shoulder to see what was happening. Maybe little groups were starting to form as a result.

When the announcement was made about the new coaching structure I thought it was fantastic the way Kempy handled himself by turning up and talking to the media. It's sad for him that he lost the job he wanted but I think Ivan will do a great job now, especially being totally in charge. I really like the idea of having Ackers as assistant coach, too. I was coached by him in development teams before the Warriors started and I think he's one of the most passionate guys in this country about rugby league. He watches so many games and he's a bloke players can go to for advice and for small pointers on football. He's probably more fatherly now I guess, while Ivan's more like a bigger brother as coach. As an older player it has been good to have a coach like Kempy where it's more like an older brother and a younger brother. When I was younger, it was more like father and son with John Monie and Frank Endacott.

Ackers has probably been a bit unlucky with his timing. He was involved with the club from the start as a colts and reserve-grade coach and might well have come up the ranks to coach the first-grade team but it never happened. Now he's much closer to the action after coming on board as the club's football development manager. Campo has been great to have back in Auckland with his attitude and his background at the club. Everyone takes notice of him and now he's also going to drive the players as the trainer, too. While Mick has been criticised for a lot of things he did, it's fair to point out he was responsible for bringing Ivan, John and Campo back to the club last year as well as signing Pricey, Ruben, Nathan and Todd.

I think John Hart's involvement in the club has been interesting since he joined the Cullen Sports board earlier in the year. He showed how passionate he was straightaway but, now that he has the job of executive director of football, I hope he'll step back and let Ivan do his job as coach without standing over him too much. Eric has obviously placed his faith in John to be his eyes and ears at the club but I don't think he should be too hands-on. He spoke to us before a couple of games and he did it well, although I wouldn't like to think that would happen too much. That needs to be the coach's job. From what I've seen so far, John's actually similar to Mick in some ways in terms of what he wanted to put in place immediately with a new structure and new appointments but it won't work if he gets too involved.

Now the club not only has Hart involved in a new coaching set-up but it also has a new CEO in Wayne Scurrah. I must say I feel sorry for Wayne because the media will always want to speak to him despite him saying he wants to keep a lower profile. That will require some work.

Apart from that, one issue he and the club need to look at — and it's one that has worried me for a long time — is the number of players who leave the Warriors. Players talk and a lot of them have been unhappy at the club for various reasons; a lot of it is to do with results but some have also been unhappy about the way they've been treated or how their mates have been treated.

What I struggle with mostly, though, is how many players went in 2005 — especially high-profile ones — and the club hasn't been able to make any big signings. I know very little pressure is put on players to stay when they say they want to go; on the other side you can always argue, why try to make them stay when they want to leave? I understand a lot of contracts would need to be stepped up and the club also went about securing a lot of our younger players, but in 2005 Iafeta Paleaaesina, Francis Meli, Monty Betham, Tevita Latu, Karl Temata and I all left and there wasn't one big signing. That's the part I have a problem with. Forgetting Steve and Ruben who came to the club as high-profile signings, I think it means some of the other players must be getting paid a hell of a lot of money if there's not room under the salary cap to buy more players.

Losing players in significant numbers is not a new thing for the Warriors, though. I've seen players being released early or not being re-signed ever since the club started. Denis Betts, Greg Alexander, Joe Vagana, Nigel Vagana, Gene Ngamu, Sean Hoppe and more were able to leave, weren't wanted or were eased out and that's just kept happening. So many players are able to go before their term is up and that's where the club and players need to be more professional. I know I finished a year earlier but that had been arranged well in advance. We've seen it with others like Monty, Francis and some of the guys who finished in 2004. There are reasons in every case but sometimes players have to bite the bullet and see it out. There are other times when players are signed on longer-term deals and the club basically shows them the door by making them feel like they should ask for a release. That's not peculiar to the Warriors or rugby league for that matter. It also happens at clubs throughout the NRL and in the English Super League.

Going to England is an attractive option for the players because of the money involved. That's been the way since New Zealanders started playing there in big numbers around 20 years ago. The contracts are way bigger than they are in the NRL. When I was younger I know I could have picked up more money playing for other clubs but my attitude was that if I stayed firm and loyal the better money would come and the club would look after me. A lot of guys are impatient and want the money now. It was a little bit disappointing that Feka left because he was young and wasn't far away from moving ahead. If he'd stuck it out for another year, he'd be able to get very good money here plus he'd be playing at home with his friends and family around, and that's something players need to look at, too. That was important to me. Then again, with Feka, I also find myself saying, good on him. The deal he has at Wigan is outstanding for him and for his family and the good thing is that he's got every chance to come back. There's no way the Warriors could afford to pay him huge money with Pricey and Rubes as the leading props. He would have been on the bench and, when you look at it like that, he probably had to go.

I've talked about some players being unhappy at the Warriors over the years. That happens at a football club. I don't think the club's a bad place to be, though. Over 11 years there were some times that weren't so good but, hell, we're better off than a lot of other people. The mood at the club is determined by the joy of winning and the disappointment of losing; there's such a huge gap between the two but really there's little to complain about when you're a professional footballer.

Taking over from 'Whiz'

Australian players are always telling us State of Origin football is the pinnacle in the game for them these days. I don't doubt them. I can see what they're on about. It's incredible to witness the intensity, competitiveness and quality of the football on offer and I can only imagine what it would be like to play an Origin match.

But, as a New Zealander, there'll never be anything to top test football for me. I can say that after playing in a grand final, which was unquestionably up there on another level from anything else in the NRL. Some of the other matches I played for the Warriors have been extraordinary for their intensity, too, and I'd say I could put a couple of our clashes against the Broncos in that category. For all that, I can't go past test footy at its best, specifically some of the matches I've played against the Kangaroos. I missed the Kiwis' 2003 win over Australia at North Harbour Stadium and the draw at the same ground in 2004 but, watching them, I was in total admiration seeing the brutality, ferocity, passion and, at the same time, skill involved.

For me, it's always easy to take my mind back to the great tests I played and none were better than a few of them against Australia. In that category I'd instantly mention the Anzac Test at North Harbour

Stadium in 1998 and the win we had there a few months earlier at the end of the 1997 season. There was just the strongest sense of togetherness and purpose, the bond I'd always felt the moment I first became a Kiwi.

That's why it was a real bonus for me to be able to finish my playing career in New Zealand with the privilege of playing for the Kiwis one last time in 2005. I certainly hadn't planned on it. I was willing to stick to my announcement in late 2004 that I had retired from international football. I know that decision came about in difficult circumstances but once the Warriors had finished their 2005 NRL season, a lot of people tried to persuade me to make myself available again. New Kiwi coach Brian McClennan asked me to reconsider, Peter Leitch had his say, so did my team-mates Ruben Wiki and Steve Price, Kiwi selector Tony Iro and former Warriors CEO Mick Watson. They all said: 'Go on, Stace, have another shot.'

I didn't want to do it for the wrong reasons. It wasn't about me. It was about helping the team. There were problems finding fit bodies to play in the halves so on that basis I was honoured to be asked and pleased to be able to say yes. It really was such a thrill to be able to join the boys again in a Kiwi camp and to do it at a time when Brian had come in as a new coach with a new organisation. I'll say it again, I love test footy and this was a chance to appreciate one last time why it means so much to all of us who play it.

I suppose there was a sense of relief about being able to do it as well. While I had agreed to make it just for the two Tri Nations tests against Australia at Telstra Stadium and Ericsson Stadium, it was rewarding to have another shot because my last test experience before that hadn't been such a good one at all. No one has any right to expect success in an international but the 2003 Anzac Test in Sydney wasn't one of the special ones. Rather than being played in April, this was scheduled for Friday, 25 July 2003. I won't forget it and I'm sure Daniel Anderson won't either. The venue was Aussie Stadium, and the following night New Zealand and Australia also clashed in a rugby union test at Telstra Stadium. I'm afraid we didn't do too well in setting the tone for a weekend of trans-Tasman sporting rivalry; thankfully the All Blacks did far better the next night. We were completely overrun 48–6 by a Kangaroo side hardened from high-quality football in the State of Origin series. It was a cruel set-up really, nothing better than an ambush.

I strained my groin after about 15 minutes and knew I was in trouble. I couldn't run, I couldn't even pass and I was having real problems making tackles as well. Early in the second half it was just pointless being out there. I wasn't helping anyone. I had to come off and Richard Swain moved to halfback from hooker. We were really light on halves and had few choices, especially with four forwards named on the interchange bench. With Richard going to halfback, we had to move Monty Betham to hooker and then, when David Vaealiki had to come off with a corked thigh, Nigel Vagana had to switch to fullback with Joe Galuvao going to one of his old spots in the centres. Just when it couldn't get any worse, Matt Utai simply walked off the field claiming he had a shoulder injury — and then turned around and played for the Bulldogs two days later, not to mention scoring a couple of tries. So we had three of us sitting on the bench not able to play and just one player left to use as an interchange option. It was hard work because I couldn't do anything. I felt so sorry for the guys out there.

The experience was just as galling for Ando. After being brought in to replace Gary Freeman, it was his debut as Kiwi coach and not an auspicious one obviously. He'd tried to make the camp work and I thought he did a decent job of it. Olsen Filipaina, the outstanding Kiwi of the late 1970s and '80s, was brought in to give the jerseys out to the players. That was a nice touch. Olsen was such a legend when he played and certainly saved his best performances for the Kiwis from everything I've learnt about his career. But how did it feel being in a Kiwi team with an Australian as coach? It was no big deal to me at the time. Ando handled things fine. He said his job was to get us to win, nothing more and nothing less.

I never played another test when Daniel was coach, though, so I find it hard to pass judgement on him. I couldn't be involved in the one at the end of the 2003 season because straight after our loss to Penrith in the NRL finals I had an operation on my ankle. Besides, my groin injury wouldn't have allowed me to play in any case. If I had been fit, I would have been available for the test. There wouldn't have been an issue at all.

By the time the 2004 Anzac Test came around, the landscape had changed. I'd made my decision to be unavailable on the back of some form issues with the Warriors and the treatment Daniel had dished out to me earlier in the season and especially after the Bulldogs game. And when the Tri Nations series rolled around at the end of the year, I'd made up my mind that I wouldn't be available for the Kiwis. A whole lot of Warriors were unavailable, mainly for injury-related reasons: Sione Faumuina needed a shoulder reconstruction; Lance Hohaia had knee surgery; Jerome Ropati was scheduled for a wrist operation and Monty Betham had some problems that needed rest. Awen Guttenbeil made a personal choice to be unavailable on the basis he believed his form wasn't up to standard for him to be considered, Clinton Toopi had an operation on his thumb but recovered to make the tour while Vinnie Anderson also toured, although he had been advised to rest a chronic injury.

Then there was my case. I just didn't feel right about playing for the Kiwis after what had happened earlier in the year so the club was going to tell the NZRL I was unavailable. I also wanted a break to freshen up after a difficult season. I hadn't played well and there'd been a lot of other outside forces that created added pressure. At the same time, the club didn't want a lot of us to go on the tour. We were told there wouldn't be a break when we returned, that we'd have to go straight into off-season training with the rest of the squad. I had that in the back of my mind as well and thought I'd rather just stay home to ensure I was in the best possible shape for the Warriors in 2005. I owed it to them.

I'd spoken to Daniel a couple of times and he'd asked me to come back into the side, but in the end I told him I definitely wouldn't be available. That's when he came back to me, ringing me up to say he wanted me to make an announcement that I was retiring from test football. He said he wanted me to do it that way because it would help him from copping a lot of crap by saying I was going to retire. That's fairly much what happened. It was in the back of my mind that retirement was something I might have to do, like Brad Fittler did when he said he was devoting all his time to the Roosters. If I did it, I was going to do it for my reasons and, when Daniel asked me, I guess that just convinced me to handle it that way. When I made the announcement I think it took a bit of heat off both of us actually. Because he suggested it to me, it made it a lot easier for me to execute.

By leaving it that way I was able to concentrate on the Warriors' preparation for the 2005 NRL season but, while the Kiwis were on tour and were having problems in the halves, the NZRL asked me to be available for one game against Great Britain. They wanted me just for a week and, while I considered it, I thought it was fairly pointless. I was just into our off-season training programme by then and wasn't in the right shape to be going over there to play in one test.

So, I really thought my time in test football had finished — until the approaches came in late in 2005. That made me stop to consider what the Kiwis had meant to me and the memories they'd given me.

It's no accident that most of the best moments of my Kiwi career can be traced back to the time when Frank Endacott reigned as coach. That's perfectly understandable because he was there the longest; therefore on the law of averages there must have been some good times. He was in just his second season in the job when I started and he didn't finish until after the 2000 World Cup. He always had the knack of making a Kiwi camp mean something to all of us and he was undoubtedly the best of the Kiwi coaches I had.

I first came into contact with Frank on a coaching level when he ran the Warriors' reserve-grade side in 1995 and, by the end of that year, I was not only a Warriors first-grader but I was in Frank's New Zealand team for the World Cup in Britain. I had no inkling he was thinking along those lines and the way I found out was quite bizarre really. I was at the airport about to fly to Sydney for an awards dinner when a television news reporter approached me to tell me I'd made the Kiwi team to go to the World Cup. I was shocked. I didn't even know the team was going to be announced then.

Tea Ropati was travelling with me and made me appreciate how special it was to be selected for the Kiwis. We had a few drinks on the plane, got to Sydney and went to the bar for a few more . . . so there was a bit of celebrating after that one.

Before going away, we went into an army camp and that's where I really met Gary Freeman, Matthew Ridge and lots of the other guys for the first time (apart from playing against them). It was a hell of a squad with a few other Warriors making it — Gene Ngamu, Stephen Kearney, Syd Eru, Hitro Okesene, Richie Blackmore and Sean Hoppe. As well as Freeman and Ridge, the side included Kevin Iro, John Lomax, Quentin Pongia, Tony Iro, Tony Kemp, Daryl Halligan, Mark Horo, Jason Williams, John Timu and Jason Lowrie among others.

Always likely to be the centre of attention whenever the Kiwis were together was Ridgey. You couldn't help but notice him. I was just this quiet little guy new to the scene and he was so loud — and angry that day we came into camp having joined us the day after his Manly side had lost the grand final to the Bulldogs. I shook hands with him, went into the room, the television was going and the news was on with a story about the grand final. Well, next thing Ridgey has just blown up, picked up a phone book and hurled it at the TV. I was sitting there not knowing what to say, where to go or what to do. That was so Ridgey. Then Daryl Halligan, John Timu and Jason Williams all turned up blind from celebrating their win with the Dogs. Wisely, they thought better of bagging him too much because Ridgey sure could do his scone. But as a trainer, competitor and influence around the team he was huge.

For me, it was a comfort having Frank and the other Warriors involved because we were used to each other being around the club all the time. Having Steve and Hitro was the biggest plus. They'd been so good to me all year at the Warriors and, once we got on tour, Hitro,

Gene, Syd and me — the new boys — made a point of sticking together, so much so the four of us were virtually sewn at the hip throughout that trip. There was very much a senior group in the Kiwis then, the back of the bus business and all that, a lot different from what it is today where there's not the same hierarchy really.

We stayed on the outskirts of Leeds but there was a village just down the road which had about 10 pubs. Early in the week Syd, Hitro, Gene and I would do a wee pub crawl around the area. As I say, the four of us made sure we were always together. Gene and I actually roomed together as well, as we did with the Warriors at that time.

As a roomie, Gene was a bit of a problem. He wasn't all that tidy. In contrast Awen Guttenbeil, my only other long-time roomie, was tidy but, man, he stank. His body odour was just shocking. Gene didn't exactly cover himself in glory the next year — 1996 — when we were touring around New Zealand playing tests against Papua New Guinea and Great Britain. After winning the third test in Christchurch, and taking the series 3–0, we had a night on the drink. Our accommodation was in a place where we had units with a little lounge and separate bedrooms. When we got home that night, Geno took all his clothes off, turned the TV on and sat down with his sunglasses on. When I woke up the next morning, I came out into the lounge and Geno was asleep in the chair with this big pile of spew on the floor beside him. The cleaners came in later and the bugger blamed it all on me. While he wasn't a tidy roomie he was a good bloke to be on tour with that first time in the Kiwis, especially when the experience was so new for both us.

It was this tournament that became known I guess for what happened to Gary Freeman. There had been no signal from Frank about my likely involvement. I had imagined I would be there as back-up for Whiz but I think Ridgey had a lot to do with me being selected for the first match against Tonga at Warrington. From what I can tell he really wanted me to be in the team and he seemed to have a big say in what went on with selection. When I was chosen, I was obviously excited. I don't think Whiz was that happy about missing out but I can't say enough about him. He made a point of congratulating me and wishing me all the best and he was always keen to provide advice; I was more than happy to listen to him with all the experience he had. As it was just the first match of the tournament, I thought Whiz would come back into halfback for the next game against Papua New Guinea.

As for my first test . . . well, it didn't go too well for us for a long time. Mike McClennan was coaching the Tongans and they had a lot of useful players. One of them was Awen with his curly top while former Kiwis Duane Mann and George Mann were there along with Solomon Haumono, Martin Masella, Tevita Vaikona and Phil Howlett (All Black Doug Howlett's brother). They were giving it to us as well when they jumped to a 24–12 lead with only eight minutes left. If something didn't happen quickly we were all in line to be part of one of the biggest shocks in rugby league history. It didn't bear thinking about.

The Tongans were revelling in it. At one stage Awen tackled me around the legs and, as I got up, he pulled my pants down. True. In the middle of a test he down-troued me and then just laughed. He was getting a bit cocky believing they would win and we had our reasons to be concerned but we put together a comeback, scored a couple of tries, Ridgey converted both from wide out to make it 24–24 and then added a field goal to win it for us. That was another one to chalk up against Awen.

When the next game came against Papua New Guinea, Whiz still wasn't halfback. I was picked there again while Gary was named at hooker. From what I could see, he didn't seem that worried about it. Syd Eru had since been banned for testing positive to pseudoephedrine so Whiz came into dummy half. He went well there, too, as we moved through to the semi-finals to play Australia. That's where trouble flared up.

We'd beaten Papua New Guinea 22–6 but instead of staying with Whiz at hooker, Frank went for Henry Paul and left Whiz out of the squad completely. He responded by staying on the team bus, none too happy about being overlooked. A lot of the guys ribbed me about taking Whiz's spot but I think he believed he was going to be hooker for that side, not halfback. It turned out his one World Cup appearance was to be his 46th and last for the Kiwis.

Before we considered playing Australia there was actually a much bigger issue to deal with and once again Ridgey was at the centre of it. Together with Mark Horo and Kempy, he'd led the campaign for better financial rewards for us. Kempy had been communicating with the Australians to find out what sort of money they were on for the tournament. Loaded with that information, our senior players had taken a case to the New Zealand Rugby League for an increase, which was, as we understood it, agreed to before we left. Trouble was, by the time we arrived in England, we were told the budget wouldn't allow what we were looking for.

I wasn't that worried about it because I was that happy to be in the team for the first time but Ridgey and the other boys weren't wearing it. So, after we had played our first two games, a meeting was organised with NZRL boss Graham Carden where senior players aired their grievances. Kempy got up and said the NZRL's offer was bullshit, Mark Horo had his say, so did Ridgey and then Henry Paul leapt up to say something. Quick as a flash Carden jumped in and said: 'Look, Henry, sit down. You've only just got here.' That was typical of Henry. If he had something to say he would and Robbie would do the same. Not me, though; I was trying to hide away in the back of the room. The players had a right to complain. We'd been promised one thing back home but were now finding the rules had changed. Ridgey wasn't prepared to accept that.

In the end, there was no sign of the NZRL agreeing so Ridgey said: 'Stuff this, we're not going to play then.' We were due to train the next morning and poor old Frank was stuck right in the middle, of course. Later Gene and I were told by management that if we didn't get on the bus for training the next day we'd never play for the Kiwis again. We were scared stiff and went to see Ridgey about it. All he could do was laugh about it, as he would. 'Don't worry about it, boys. They won't do that to you,' he told us.

When we went downstairs the next morning, the only person sitting in the bus ready to go was Frank. We weren't dressed ready for training and we all just walked straight past the bus. The senior guys were still trying to sort out our tactics over the money issue but eventually the NZRL ended the standoff by coming back with an improved offer. We were always going to play the game. There was never any danger we wouldn't and I'm sure it never affected the way we prepared for the game either. It was simply something Ridgey stood up for on behalf of the team.

Our semi-final against the Australians was an awesome match, my first example of why test football at its best is so special. This was the match the Kangaroos led 14–4 at halftime and 20–6 soon after but we poured it on late as first Richie Barnett and then Tony Iro scored to trim the margin to 20–16. With minutes to go Kevin Iro got across wide out to make it 20–20 but Ridgey, such a good goalkicker, wasn't close with the chance to win the match. It was probably the worst conversion attempt of his whole career. Even then we still had time for one last attempt to snatch victory when Ridgey had a shot at a left-footed field goal. It was just wide and in extra time Australia settled it with two tries to win 30–20. It was still a fantastic match, though, unlike anything I'd been involved in before.

A taste of being New Zealanders all together in a test team in 1995 had me hoping for more in years to come. Of the 36 tests I played, I was involved against the Kangaroos more than any other side and the ratio of wins to losses was never what we wanted it to be; at least there were wins, though, and there are a lot of decent players who wore the Kiwi jersey but never experienced success against the toughest of our foes.

Of three series against Great Britain, two were won and the other squared. One I really enjoyed was the 1996 campaign in New Zealand, not simply because we swept it 3–0 but because it was a series that took us around New Zealand. Coming after the Warriors had finished business for the year, we had a sequence of five tests with two against Papua New Guinea first — in Rotorua and Palmerston North — followed by three against the Brits in Auckland, Palmerston

North and Christchurch. It was brilliant being on the road and going to other centres around the country.

Especially satisfying in 1996 was the 3–0 series score-line, especially for the guys who had been on the 1993 tour when Great Britain whitewashed the Kiwis. That was still fresh and to be able to avenge that result meant a lot to them. It was a bit of a mission winning the first two tests 17–12 (John Timu scored our two tries) and 18–15 (Ruben Wiki with two tries then), but the effort was far more complete when we rolled the Brits 32–16 at Lancaster Park.

Again in the Great Britain team then was a player New Zealanders had come to know rather well, but not because they admired him that much. That was my opposite Bobby Goulding, who now spelt his first name Bobbie for whatever reason. He'd caused a fair bit of strife when he'd toured previously but I didn't think he was that bad in this series. He was a tough competitor but still a bit of a pest with it. I remember in one of the tests I was lying on the ground and Goulding ran back and just stomped on my ankle for no apparent reason. I looked up at him and thought: 'I hope we win this one because of you.'

That's not the kind of idiotic behaviour you'd expect of Stephen Kearney. As I have said, he was one of the most professional players I was involved with. He was someone you could talk to about anything, especially to seek advice. He looked after himself and never left anything to chance in what he ate, how he trained — just everything. He'd have a couple of beers but never over the top, not when he was in-season as such. He exercised total control throughout the year and on tour, maybe letting his hair down a bit when it was all over.

On the other hand, another of my regular Kiwi team-mates was a hard, hard man — Quentin Pongia. He was a good bloke and a joy to play behind for a halfback like me. He trained hard, played hard and drank hard but, on the last of those scores, no one could match Sponge (Tony Iro). He would have to be the biggest drinker I ever came across in my time, just a legend who could handle it so well, too. Not a bad player, either. He just had so many skills and great pace for a man of his size.

Ruben Wiki was someone who commanded so much respect almost the moment he made the Kiwi team. Even when he was young he seemed to be seen as a senior player. I can say without hesitation that of everyone I've played with, he was the one who had the greatest passion for and pride in playing for New Zealand. Rubes is one who often talks about the family feeling around the Kiwis and that's so true, especially touring Britain when it was just us, so far from home and all banded together with a common purpose.

One of the game's great players I had an involvement with only briefly in the Kiwis was Tawera Nikau. He made just one test appearance during my career — against Australia in 1997 — because of the differences he had with Richie Blackmore. Richie wasn't back for the Anzac Test so the way was cleared for Tawera to play for the first and only time since 1994. It was great having him there. He walked straight into the side and was immediately a senior player despite having been away from the scene for quite a while. He had such mana about him and gave out plenty of advice. He had his reasons for not playing but you could see there was enormous pride once he was back in the side.

That test wasn't such a good one, though. We were beaten 34–22 after being well down at halftime but the return match at North Harbour Stadium was dazzling. It was the first time we'd played there, only my third test against the Australians and already I was in a Kiwi side that had beaten them. It was a trouncing really as we won 30–12, one of New Zealand's biggest winning margins in history against Australia.

It only got better, too, because just a few months later we were back at the same ground for the Anzac Test, the first of a three-test series that would be completed at the end of the season. The Australians probably tried their best to brush off the effort in 1997 because it was a Super League side we played but in 1998, with the game unified again, they couldn't complain. Just about all the big names were there — Brad Fittler, Laurie Daley as the captain, Andrew Johns, Wendell Sailor, Steve Renouf, Paul Harragon, Glenn Lazarus . . . it was a heck of a side. Typically, we weren't given much show either.

Steve Kearney was suspended, Gene Ngamu, Syd Eru and Tony Puletua were all out injured and then, with the match barely under way, we lost John Lomax with a neck problem, leaving us to play out the match with a three-man bench. When we were 12–2 down close to halftime it probably seemed grim but the first of Kevin Iro's two tries meant we went to the break only 12–6 down. In the second half we just shifted into another gear. The physical confrontations were plain fearsome. Of all the tests I played in, this must have been the most physically bruising of them all as we finished over the top of the Aussies to win 22–16.

In the lead-up to the test, Brad Thorn had gone on about how he wanted to become an All Black. Ridgey gave him a sledge about that during the match saying: 'You'll never be an All Black!' Good at the time but we all know that one did work out for Thorn in the end. Probably the biggest feature, though, was the game Darren Lockyer had. He came off the bench after Robbie O'Davis was injured early and he just couldn't do a thing right. We kicked low to him and he made a heap of errors.

In that test we had three players home from their English clubs — Robbie Paul from Bradford, Henry Paul from Wigan and Richie Blackmore from Leeds. It worked that time but I'd have to say the idea of using English-based players in tests down here generally doesn't work. There's just not enough time to prepare, not enough time to get over the effects of the travel. I've seen it fail too often, none worse than the 2000 Anzac Test when we were savaged 52–0 in Sydney. Henry and Robbie were back for that one but they were lucky to have one run with the team. The outcome was our worst defeat in history and certainly the worst match I played in. I also saw the most sickening sight I've seen in a game when Richie Barnett had his face smashed in a frightening head clash with Wendell Sailor.

After we'd won the Anzac Test in 1998, we were in a position to possibly win the series but, unfortunately, we couldn't match it in the second test later in the year in Brisbane or in the decider back at North Harbour Stadium. So we were still without a series win against Australia since 1953 but two wins in a row against them wasn't so bad.

That became three wins in three years when the Tri Nations series was held in New Zealand and Australia in late 1999. The Kiwis, Australia and Great Britain played each other once with the top two teams meeting in the final. By the time we opened the competition against the Kangaroos it was 15 October and a lot of us had been out of football for quite a few weeks.

What we did have, though, were three players from Melbourne's grand final-winning team — Stephen Kearney, Richard Swain and Matt Rua — and we were also able to field a combination that was strong across the park. Richie Barnett was at fullback, Nigel Vagana and Lesley Vainikolo on the wings, Ruben Wiki and Willie Talau in the centres, Robbie Paul and me in the halves with a front row of Joe Vagana, Henry Paul and Craig Smith plus Kearney, Rua and Logan Swann in the back row. The interchange players were David Kidwell, Jason Lowrie, Nathan Cayless and Swain. Added to that, Russell Smith was again the referee and we seemed to go fairly well when he was in charge.

Playing in front of 21,000 at Ericsson Stadium, we made an absolutely electric start to the match playing some exceptional football to score four tries — all converted — and lead 24–4 at halftime. Then our lack of football started to catch up and we had to hang really tough to hold the Aussies off to win 24–22. For me, that was the end of the series, though. A week later I had my left arm broken playing against Tonga and missed our match against Great Britain — which the boys won — and then the final against the Aussies. That was heartbreaking. We were leading 20–18 after Nigel scored late only for Wendell Sailor to grab the match-winner in the dying stages.

Predictably enough, I played against Australia more than any other country — 15 of my 36 tests — while there were nine tests against Great Britain spread over three separate series. Having been part of a 3–0 blitz in 1996, we were keen for a repeat in England in 1998 and we went so close after edging to a 22–16 win in the first test at Huddersfield and creaming the Brits 36–16 at Bolton. Then, when we were ahead 23–16 in the third at Vicarage Road in London — the home of the Watford Football Club — we allowed the home side to sneak a 23–23 draw with a try and a late field goal. Not many teams win 3–0 in Britain but we should have. Still, that was probably my favourite tour because it was three successive tests and didn't go on too long. It was also another trip when Gene and I invested in a car to run around in, this time a green Ford Escort, which was probably marginally better than the VW that gassed us in 1997.

When we were back in that part of the world for the 2000 World Cup, the tour was a bit strung out because there were a lot of preliminary matches against Lebanon, Cook Islands and Wales in our pool, a quarter-final against France, a semi-final against England and then the final against Australia at Old Trafford. We killed England 49–6 and actually stuck with the Aussies for a long time in the final only to fade in the last 20 minutes and lose 40–12.

Frank finished up as Kiwi coach after that final. I'd always enjoyed playing for him because he made you feel so special about playing for New Zealand. He certainly had a long time in the job and, under him, I had a part in all sorts of successes — we'd beaten Australia three times and that's no mean feat, we'd taken two series against Great Britain and made the 2000 World Cup final. I played in 25 tests under him and our record was outstanding with 17 wins, a draw and only seven losses (all of those to Australia).

So, when it was time for a new coach I thought Graeme Norton was a little unlucky not to take over. I played in New Zealand teams with him when we won the World Nines title twice. Instead, Whiz was appointed when perhaps he might have been given the job a little later after gaining more coaching experience. I think that was shown up when he was given only two years in the job.

There was just a test against France and one against Australia in his first year in charge while in 2002 we had an end-of-season test against the Kangaroos in Wellington — one we really should have won but lost 32–24 — and then a tour to Britain and France. It was ridiculous having the test against Australia so soon after playing for the Warriors in the grand final. There were only five days between the two games, which was stupid; I really don't know how we managed to front up in the test — and yet we were in a position to win it.

The tour provided me with one of my greatest honours when I was named as captain of a Kiwi team for a tour to Britain and France while a total of 11 Warriors made the team. After the season we'd had I had difficulty, though, with the number of games involved. While there were tests against Wales and France as well as three against Great Britain, we also faced Hull FC, St Helens and England A. I actually felt a bit homesick as well because it was an odd experience being captain on a tour like that. You have a room to yourself and I found it a bit lonely, not having someone around you to watch television with and just chat to.

The tour had its challenges. Whiz was good fun to be on tour with but I think he and assistant coach Gerard Stokes didn't work all that well together and, of course, there was the major concern about Whiz not replacing injured players on tour. Of the 26 players originally named, three didn't travel — Nathan Cayless, Andrew Lomu and Matt Utai — and they weren't replaced. Once on tour we lost Steve Kearney, who had to return home early for family reasons, Motu Tony was injured and so were a few others but no replacements were called in.

Gary spoke to me as well as Ruben Wiki about the possibility of bringing in a replacement player at one point. He told us he wanted to call up Wairangi Koopu. We backed him and Whiz said he was going to ring him right away. I think Clinton was within earshot at the time and heard what was going on. Well, he rang Wai and told him to pack his bags before Whiz had made contact. An hour later Whiz came back to us and said he'd changed his mind, that he thought he had enough cover. Clinton's thinking: 'Oh, no. What have I done?' I think Clinton turned his phone off after that. Poor Wai, he never did get that call.

Of course, Clinton had dramas of his own when he had a scuffle with Nigel Vagana. We were all in a bar and something happened. I don't know what. Clinton used to drink then — he doesn't now

— and he could get a bit fiery. Nigel was an easy-going bloke and you wouldn't expect him to get too upset so something obviously went on. They had a bit of a set-to, leaving Toops with a broken wrist and an early trip home. It meant we were down to only six fit backs so Sean Hoppe was whistled up for a test comeback.

I was curious about Gary's attitude on replacements. I thought we definitely needed some reinforcements after losing so many players. When I asked Whiz about his theory on no replacements, he said he felt if he had too many players there, there would be blokes who wouldn't be getting any football and they'd be unhappy about it.

I'm sure that cost us in the end, though. We'd won the first test fairly well 30–16 and drew 14–14 in the second but found ourselves short on troops by the time the series decider came around. Losing Steve and Clinton at that late stage — Steve had to rush home to be with his wife and daughter — was a killer. What upset us even more, though, was the decision over who should hold the Albert Baskiville Trophy. This had been donated for series between the two sides for the first time but it was decided by someone in the NZRL that the first holders should be the winners of the third test. Quite why, I don't know. The series finished up level and we should have shared the trophy. It wasn't something we should have gifted like that. It was a sour end to the series.

After that it still wasn't over — there was one more match to play and, while I didn't know it then, it took me to the place that is about to become my new home for the next two years. Our destination was Perpignan and a one-off test against France, one of the last tests of my career. It was a match that gave us an anticipated 36–10 win and provided me with my 14th and 15th test tries. It would be nice to think the strike rate will continue with Les Catalans during my stay in the south of France over the next two years.

Simply the best . . .

So there you have it, 11 years and 238 games in the NRL plus 36 tests. It's a reasonable amount of football and I guess that total should be boosted by another 60 or so appearances with Les Catalans in the English Super League in 2006.

Put it that way and it's also obvious I've played alongside and against countless players at NRL and international level. In my time at the Warriors alone, I'm one of 125 players who have worn the club's colours in 11 years. Above all, I've been privileged to play at a time when rugby league has been blessed by the presence of some of the best players the game has and will ever see, such as Alfie Langer, Darren Lockyer, Brad Fittler and especially Andrew Johns. The others have had some freakish skills but Joey is just in outer space compared to everyone else.

With that combination of games played and players seen, the pressure has gone on. Playing selector isn't a job I picked for myself. I'm dead scared of leaving someone out, someone, that is, who thinks they should have been picked. But I don't have any real choice. I've been told, not asked, to play the game and look at naming my best or favourites during my career.

I'm also under orders in one other regard. I've been told there's no need to select a halfback in either my best Warriors or Kiwis teams. You're it Stacey, they've told me.

That goes against the grain because I'm not big on picking myself in a team. Then again, it has been pointed out to me that very few other players have worn the No 7 jersey for either New Zealand or the Warriors from 1995 to 2005. When the Warriors first started, Greg Alexander had a few games there, Gene Ngamu was even used in the position and, when I missed the start of the 2000 season after breaking my arm, hooker Robbie Mears and Ben Lythe played halfback. After that Lance Hohaia, PJ Marsh and Thomas Leuluai have had some exposure but, because I missed only 20-odd matches after my debut, no one had a real crack at it. The same has applied with the Kiwis, even more so actually. So I'm the halfback in those two sides.

When we thought about this as an exercise there was something I liked immediately. My teams would look perfect on paper but no one would ever be able to find out because they'd never play. That makes winning as certain as it is whenever I take Awen on at anything. He knows he can't beat me — and he had the cheek to call me his whipping boy at my testimonial lunch in Auckland. One thing's certain: he'll pay for it. He just doesn't have any idea when that will be.

Now we have this business of picking a few best-of combinations covering the years 1995–2005 when I played in the NRL and at test level. One will be the best Warriors line-up I can come up with — and I'll do everything I can to leave Awen out (that won't be difficult) — while I'm going to have a shot at the best Kiwi line-up and a combination made up of the cream of the NRL.

I might even come up with a top referee if I can think of one (of course I can, Billy).

This great competition has been the NRL since 1998 now; that's when the ARL and Super League ended rugby league's dirty war, settled their differences and came up with the great compromise.

Before that we had the Winfield Cup in 1995, the Optus Cup in 1996 and Super League's Telstra Cup in 1997. I can't say enough about the competition, whatever it has been called. Only in 1997 when the game was split was there a problem. That wasn't surprising. We were in the Super League camp and had just 10 clubs in total, including a few that never lasted like Adelaide, Perth and Hunter.

That same year the ARL had a 12-team comp and some of those went west as well (North Sydney, Gold Coast and South Queensland) while others merged.

As a player in the game from 1995 to 2005 I couldn't have been more spoiled. The quality of players through that period was unbelievable. I missed out crossing paths with a couple of the best we've ever seen, Mal Meninga and Wally Lewis. They'd finished by the time I started, Meninga just the year before. It didn't matter too much, though, because the list of names I came across during my career just goes on and on.

Ricky Stuart, Bradley Clyde, Glenn Lazarus, Paul Harragon, Steve Renouf, Steve Walters and Andrew Ettingshausen were among those in circulation during the earlier part of my career. In picking my NRL side, though, I've looked at players whose careers span the entire 1995–2005 time frame or at least come very close to it. When you start researching, it's a tribute to those players to find how many of them have survived that length of time in a competition that's as relentless as this one.

As it happens, almost all of them have also experienced grand-final success at least once and naturally all of them have played international football.

At the Warriors, I've been part of teams that have had outstanding players in any year you care to pick and, in my time in the Kiwis, there have been so many wonderful players, too. The major regret was the effect suspensions and injuries had on selection. In the 36 tests I played we were almost always without first-choice players.

I'd hate to think what the Kiwis might have done if our best had been available regularly.

Stacey's best — Kiwis

So let's have a look at this. I want to start with the Kiwis for the obvious reason I've played the most important football of my life for my country alongside guys with a common bond and desire. There were some massive games for the Warriors — not least the grand final, naturally — but there was nothing to match the best tests I played in against Australia. Some of them were just brutal but they were also the supreme test of heart, mind and will.

Fullback — There were really only two main fullbacks and two exceptional ones with very different qualities — Matthew Ridge and Richie Barnett. Others like Henry Paul, Robbie Paul and David Vaealiki have been used in the No 1 jersey but not with the same regularity as Ridge and Barnett. And when I returned to the Kiwis for two final appearances this year, our adopted 'New Zealander' Brent Webb had the job and will undoubtedly have it for a long time. I needed a goalkicker — and it's not going to be me — so that makes the fullback choice easy. It's Ridge.

Wingers — There are a few to pick from here with Sean Hoppe standing out while Barnett, Daryl Halligan, Francis Meli, Lesley Vainikolo, Matt Utai, Jason Williams, Henry Fa'afili and Brian Jellick have been among the specialist wingers used in my time. We've had centres or utilities used as test wingers, too, like Nigel Vagana, Clinton Toopi and Marc Ellis. One winger has to be Hoppe, an out-and-out specialist and holder of the record for most test tries for the Kiwis with 17. While a few others were close, I can't go past Barnett. He could be used at centre, winger or fullback so he provides cover, as well, for injuries.

Centres — This is one of the most difficult selection areas because we've had a lot of excellent centres. Ruben Wiki was there when I started before he moved towards the forwards. I'm sticking with him as a forward for this team. I've also played alongside Nigel Vagana in a lot of tests both as a centre and winger but for sheer talent and strength the best to me was always Kevin Iro. Clinton Toopi was as good as anyone on his day while also on the list of possibilities are Willie Talau, John Timu, Richie Blackmore, David Vaealiki and Tonie Carroll. That's a fair collection but my vote is with Iro and Vagana.

Standoff — For a decent stretch of my career my regular team-mate Gene Ngamu wore the No 6 jersey, as did my future Warriors coach Tony Kemp when I started out as a test player. I've also been paired with Henry Paul, Robbie Paul, Lance Hohaia and Tasesa Lavea. Ngamu ran a side well, provided a kicking game and a goal-kicking option but, unfortunately for him, he was up against two special talents in the Paul brothers. They both have to be in this side somewhere so I go for Robbie at No 6.

Halfback — No discussions required here — I'm the halfback.

Props — Here's a position the Kiwis have never had a problem filling. Let's reel off some of the names to think about — Quentin Pongia, John Lomax, Jason Lowrie, Brent Stuart, Terry Hermansson, Joe Vagana, Craig Smith, Ruben Wiki, Jerry Seuseu, Nathan Cayless, Paul Rauhihi, Jason Cayless and Roy Asotasi. It's very difficult to narrow this down but a halfback more than any player appreciates the value of his props. Wiki is fantastic there but I can get around this one because he has also been a brilliant back-row forward and that's where I'm using him. That leaves me going for Pongia, one of the hardest men I played with, and Smith, who was always an all-round prop of the highest quality.

Hooker — We've had two specialists who were used extensively in my time, Syd Eru at the start of my career and Richard Swain for quite a stretch later on. They were totally reliable and did the hooker's job really well. I have a problem, though. The most talented player to run at hooker during my career was undoubtedly Henry Paul. He was capable of playing either standoff or fullback as well but I'm well-served there and Henry, like Robbie, just has to be in my side. He's my No 9.

Second-rowers — Like props, New Zealand league has had a wealth of fantastic second-rowers. When I started out we had Stephen Kearney, Tony Iro and Mark Horo at the 1995 World Cup. Quentin was also used there at the time. Eventually we had Jarrod McCracken and Wiki — when they moved in from the centres — plus the likes of Logan Swann, Tony Puletua, Joe Galuvao, Matt Rua, Ali Lauitiiti, Awen Guttenbeil, David Kidwell and David Solomona. Good as many of them are, this one is still straightforward in terms of a starting line-up — I'd have Wiki and Kearney.

Loose forward — I suppose it's fair to say the Kiwis have been short on what could be regarded as genuine loose forwards, although the position's demands have changed in the past decade as well. We have a fantastic talent now in Sonny Bill Williams if we can get him on the paddock. I haven't played with him so he misses the cut. We've tended to push second-rowers into the No 13 jersey. I've seen Kemp used there for the Kiwis as well as Mark Horo, Tyran Smith, Ruben, Stephen Kearney, Awen, Monty Betham and, more often than not, Logan. He's my man.

Interchange — I guess this becomes the best of those I couldn't squeeze into starting positions. I'd have two props — Nathan Cayless and Joe Vagana — and I'd definitely have Tony Iro in there for his impact. For my fourth reserve I'd select Blackmore to give me an option in the centres and on the wing. There's plenty of cover for every position in this line-up.

Captain — While I had the pleasure of captaining the Kiwis, that wouldn't be my job. I've gone for Ridge, who was so fiercely competitive in every team he played in and certainly when he was a team-mate in the Kiwis. There are other Kiwi captains in here, too, in Wiki, Kearney, Pongia, Barnett and Cayless.

STACEY'S BEST — KIWIS TEAM

Fullback:	Matthew Ridge (c)
Winger:	Sean Hoppe
Centre:	Nigel Vagana
Centre:	Kevin Iro
Winger:	Richie Barnett
Standoff:	Robbie Paul
Halfback:	Stacey Jones
Prop:	Quentin Pongia
Hooker:	Henry Paul
Prop:	Craig Smith
Second-rower:	Ruben Wiki
Second-rower:	Stephen Kearney
Loose forward:	Logan Swann
Interchange:	Nathan Cayless
	Joe Vagana
	Tony Iro
	Richie Blackmore

Stacey's best — Warriors

As I said, 125 players have appeared for the Warriors in my 11 years with the club, with only a handful I didn't actually play alongside at first-grade level. In sorting out my best club line-up, there's just one condition — all players must have played a reasonable length of time for the Warriors, at least two seasons.

I thought that was the fairest way to do it. In just one year, we've all seen how impressive Ruben Wiki (19 games) and Steve Price (16 games) have been for the club and right from the outset our first captain, Dean Bell was obviously superb.

He made only 19 appearances, though, so I'm disregarding all three of them for the purposes of this process.

Fullback — There are three strong prospects here, most obviously the incumbent Brent Webb (81 matches), 2000–02 fullback and now Warriors coach Ivan Cleary and former captain Matthew Ridge. Greg Alexander and Phil Blake also spent time in the No 1 jersey. Webb has a lot of great qualities and so did Ridge but I'll settle for Cleary (53 games), who was such a key for us in our best years.

Wingers — We've had a collection of wingers who have been extensively used, none more so than Francis Meli (60 tries in 110 games), Henry Fa'afili (38 tries in 94 games), Sean Hoppe (44 tries in 88 games) and Lee Oudenryn (23 tries in 61 matches). A guy like Justin Murphy was also around for a while and we also used former All Blacks John Kirwan and Marc Ellis on the wing regularly in the early years. I've settled for the two most prolific tryscorers — Meli and Hoppe.

Centres — There's a good-sized group to choose from. Clinton Toopi and Tea Ropati stand out from both ends of the club's history with Nigel Vagana in the middle. To them can be added Vinnie Anderson, John Carlaw, Anthony Swann, Richie Blackmore and also Sione Faumuina who has played a share of his 71 Warriors matches in the centres. It's hard to top genuine experience, though, so Toopi (119 matches, 56 tries) and Ropati (72 matches, 26 tries) are the choices.

Standoff — Now I have a dilemma. I'll admit this comes down to mates as well. I spent a lot of time with Gene Ngamu and Greg Alexander in the earlier part of my Warriors career — but now I have to choose between them for the No 6 spot. They're not the only contenders. I've also considered Motu Tony, Lance Hohaia and John Simon who all had something to offer. So I'm picking . . . okay, Gene, on the basis he was with the club a lot longer (81 games). Sorry, Brandy.

Halfback — For this selection, look at my Kiwi team.

Props — This is like the Kiwis. There's so much choice. Price and Wiki are out of the frame for this and so is Quentin Pongia, who also had just one season at the club. Still, who could complain when you have a list that includes Terry Hermansson, Hitro Okesene, Iafeta Paleaaesina, Jerry Seuseu, Mark Tookey, Joe Vagana and Richard Villasanti? When it comes to the starting choices, I don't find it too difficult, though — Seuseu (132 games) and Vagana with 115 games.

Hooker — This is definitely another difficult one. Syd Eru was there for a long time earlier on and Robbie Mears also had a good run in 1999–2000 while Monty Betham played there a fair bit, too. For me, though, it comes down to Jason Death (56 games), or PJ Marsh (35 games). Death was fantastic but he also played loose forward while I played my best football when Marsh was hooker so I've gone for him.

Second-rowers — This is getting too difficult now. Look at the players to choose from — Awen Guttenbeil, Stephen Kearney, Ali Lauitiiti, Logan Swann, Denis Betts, Mark Horo, Wairangi Koopu and Tony Tatupu. They all have credentials, although I've narrowed it down to a choice between Guttenbeil, Kearney, Lauitiiti, Swann and Koopu, settling for Guttenbeil (147 games) and Kearney (79). I couldn't bring myself to leave you out, Awen. I wouldn't want you sulking.

Loose forward — In all honesty, this selection is as straightforward as they come. I'll mention some others who figure as possibilities — Tony Tuimavave, Death, Kearney, Swann, Betham, Faumuina, Guttenbeil and Koopu. There's one obvious name I've left out because he's my runaway selection and that's Campo (Kevin Campion), who was with the club just two seasons, playing 44 games, but he was the best for the job.

Interchange — I've gone for an unconventional bench with all forwards and no specialist prop. Lauitiiti would be the man to help in the front row. He played there a bit, especially in 2001, and Tuimavave can also help out there. Together with Betham, Tuimavave gives me two really tough forwards to come off the bench, Monty also covering hooker (he also told me I had to pick him or I'd be in trouble when Les Catalans play Wakefield). No one I played with was more passionate about the Warriors than Monty. Koopu provides coverage at centre, as he has done from time to time.

Captain — If Awen's career hadn't been so affected by injuries early on, I think he would have become an excellent long-term captain of the Warriors. So, he's the man for me.

STACEY'S BEST — WARRIORS TEAM

Fullback:	Ivan Cleary
Winger:	Sean Hoppe
Centre:	Tea Ropati
Centre:	Clinton Toopi
Winger:	Francis Meli
Standoff:	Gene Ngamu
Halfback:	Stacey Jones
Prop:	Jerry Seuseu
Hooker:	P J Marsh
Prop:	Joe Vagana
Second-rower:	Awen Guttenbeil (c)
Second-rower:	Stephen Kearney
Loose forward:	Kevin Campion
Interchange:	Ali Lauitiiti
	Monty Betham
	Wairangi Koopu
	Tony Tuimavave

Stacey's best — NRL

This is the last and probably most difficult part of the assignment because there are just endless possibilities. In some respects, there's no room for argument. Darren Lockyer, Laurie Daley, Brad Fittler, Andrew Johns, Danny Buderus, Shane Webcke, Gorden Tallis and Alfie Langer were certainties because they're so far ahead of the field, but it was still a battle sorting through the names.

Fullback — After my 11 years in the NRL there could be only one fullback and that's Darren Lockyer. If he played there now, he'd still be the best but Brisbane, Queensland and Australia have more need for him at No 6 these days. At the same time, others should be mentioned such Anthony Minichiello, Billy Slater and Brett Mullins.

Wingers — This has always been a strange area for Australian rugby league. Quite often centres have been converted into wingers when picking the Kangaroos or the Origin teams. Minichiello, originally a winger, is a candidate here and so are Michael Hancock, Mat Rogers and Lote Tuqiri but my picks are Wendell Sailor, even though he's now out of the game, and Matt Sing, who adds so much with his all-round value.

Centres — Forget about one of the spots. That belongs to Daley. The others in the mix are Andrew Ettingshausen, Steve Renouf and Ryan Girdler while Mark Gasnier has obvious skills. Rather than an Australian, though, I'm going Kiwi by choosing Nigel Vagana, who did well with the Warriors but went to another level when he signed with the Bulldogs and has done the same at Cronulla. Just look at his record — 122 tries in 190 first-grade matches.

Standoff — It's like Lockyer at fullback. There's Brad Fittler and then there's the rest. Daley was great at No 6, though, and so is Lockyer right now as well as Trent Barrett. From the earlier years, Cliff Lyons and Kevin Walters were two of the best in the business but Fittler had no peer.

Halfback — In a field of tremendous quality there is again only one choice in Joey Johns. You just marvel at everything he does. That's tough on a great player like Alfie Langer while others who've left an impression include Greg Alexander, Ricky Stuart, Geoff Toovey, Craig Gower, Brett Kimmorley and Matt Orford.

Props — Again I've been privileged to see a prop as good as any the game has known and that's Shane Webcke. For a decade I saw another outstanding prop in opposition colours; in 2005 I had him as a team-mate — Steve Price. Other ones to list include Ruben Wiki, Glenn Lazarus, Quentin Pongia, Paul Harragon, Petero Civoniceva and Robbie Kearns while, of the newer breed, there's Luke Bailey and Jason Ryles.

Hooker — Put down the glasses — Danny Buderus wins this without a problem. However, Steve Walters and Luke Priddis stand out as very good No 9s while Johns and Gower were equally good when they were played in that position.

Second-rowers — The starting point is Gorden Tallis and then work from there. The Australians have produced Steve Menzies, Nathan Hindmarsh, Ben Kennedy and Craig Fitzgibbon as a few who stand out but New Zealand has also had some prominent second-rowers in the NRL such Kearney, Lauitiiti, Puletua and Wiki. I can't say enough about Wiki and Kearney, so Kearney's my other second-rower.

Loose forward — Menzies and Kennedy come under consideration here and so, too, from earlier years does Bradley Clyde. Here again, though, I'm going to keep it Kiwi. For my money, Wiki is my No 13 in my best NRL side.

Interchange — I couldn't shift out Joey to give Alfie the No 7 jersey so the little Queenslander is on the bench instead. My bench prop is Kearns who has been such a solid performer for years and I've partnered Langer and Kearns with two back-row options in Kennedy and Menzies.

Captain — There are captains everywhere in this side — Lockyer, Daley, Fittler, Johns, Buderus, Price, Kearney, Tallis and Wiki plus Langer, Kearns and Menzies on the bench. After having a season with him at the Warriors, I can't say enough about Price as a leader so he's the one.

STACEY'S BEST — NRL TEAM

Fullback:	Darren Lockyer
Winger:	Matt Sing
Centre:	Nigel Vagana
Centre:	Laurie Daley
Winger:	Wendell Sailor
Standoff:	Brad Fittler
Halfback:	Andrew Johns
Prop:	Shane Webcke
Hooker:	Danny Buderus
Prop:	Steve Price (c)
Second-rower:	Stephen Kearney
Second-rower:	Gorden Tallis
Loose forward:	Ruben Wiki
Interchange:	Allan Langer
	Ben Kennedy
	Robbie Kearns
	Steve Menzies

I said I'd mention a favourite referee as well. Like most players I had moments with the refs when I didn't always keep calm. I'm not going to rave on about them now. I'm over it — I think. What I would say is hardly new, though. Bill Harrigan was easily the best of the lot. The others weren't close to him. I'd have him controlling any ultimate encounter of the game's greatest names.

Thankfully, that selection task is over. I'm bound to have offended a few players. If I did I'm sorry. So many of you deserve to be chosen but it's a challenge to wedge so many names into 17 spots. What I do know is that I've had the most amazing 11 years playing for the Warriors and the Kiwis. I've finished without the premiership victory I dreamed of; at least I played in a grand final, though, and there are a lot of fantastic players who never even made it that far.

Apart from coaches and players, one constant throughout my career has, of course, been off the field, working with the media. When you play this game at this level, it's a big part of your life. There are a lot of people I want to thank for the job they did and the way they went about it in both the good and not so good times. Allen McLaughlin, Murray Deaker, Peter Ropati, Stephen McIvor and Doug Golightly were around throughout and were always great to deal with. Peter Jessup did a good job most of the time for the *New Zealand Herald* but he lost me when I was at my low point in 2004, saying I had no future at the Warriors or anywhere else. That was uncalled for.

When it came down to it, though, playing the game and not the media was what mattered most. There were just so many great moments with the Warriors and playing for my country. I relished every victory we had over Australia but there just weren't enough of them, nor was there the series win we all craved. They're the disappointments, and big ones, too, but they can't detract from the life rugby league has given me and my family. Despite many troughs, the Warriors gave me a purpose in life and developed the strongest sense of loyalty in me. I was paid well to be a Warrior, it was my job to be one but my passion for and pride in the club — and my team-mates — was always there and always will be. It would have been so easy to give up and move on somewhere else. I'm glad I chose not to.

I've played my last match in the NRL and my last test for the Kiwis. Soon I'll leave New Zealand, too. Of course I'll miss the only two teams I've played for over the last 11 years but I'm going on to a new adventure with Les Catalans in France, one I hope will be every bit as rewarding as my time has been in the game so far. That can't be guaranteed but what is a dead-set certainty is that I will be home again soon — no longer a player but glad to be back where the heart is. What won't change will be my love for the game. For me it's footy for life.

The final farewells

Dame Nelly Melba knew a thing or two about comebacks and, while it wasn't intended, Stacey Jones now knows plenty about sporting farewells. It's just as well the little man from Auckland doesn't allow emotions to run wild because he would have been spent after the last few weeks of his rugby league-playing days in New Zealand.

Phlegmatic as he may seem, though, Jones confesses he needed more than a modicum of self-control to retain his composure at least once during the string of send-offs that came his way before and after his last days with the Warriors.

He was fêted in the full gamut of ways to mark a supreme sporting performer's contribution and the first of them came when Lion Breweries produced a special batch of its Lion Red brew with a bottle emblazoned with a Stacey Jones label. It was Lion's way of farewelling a nation's special hero. Stacey was chuffed rather than tearful that day.

He was just a little stunned when *Player* magazine turned its August issue into a Stacey Jones farewell tribute, devoting not just the cover but a phenomenal amount of editorial space to a man who had so captivated a nation's people.

Even in front of almost 900 people at his testimonial luncheon at Ellerslie Convention Centre the oft-proclaimed Little General was in command and in control of his faculties as one speaker after another paid tribute to him before Awen Guttenbeil brought him back down several rungs. Maybe, just maybe, there was a lump building in the throat and certainly some goose bumps when Ruben Wiki led some of his team-mates in a haka that afternoon.

The public didn't see it but in the Warriors' inner sanctum, the dressing room, Jones was visibly affected as he addressed his team-mates before his last NRL match at Ericsson Stadium. Yes, the eyes moistened before he ran into his theatre of dreams to face Newcastle and later, sadly in defeat, walked around the ground to acknowledge the fans, his fans. There was no choking then, though, but instead obvious disappointment that the night hadn't worked out the way it ought to have.

One week he said goodbye to his rugby league constituency. Seven nights later he was in enemy territory doing the same to the NRL period by scything through in storybook style to score the Warriors' match-winning try in his 238th and last appearance. And yet his final act on the field was anything but expressive. Rather, with the score 22–20 and the final seconds ticking down, his last deed was to instinctively, calmly and professionally kick the ball into the Brookvale Oval crowd to close the contest out.

Back in the dressing room the emotion dripped, for other players there that night were also finishing — Monty Betham, Iafeta Paleaaesina, Francis Meli and Karl Temata, too. Both CEO Mick Watson, who had just resigned, and outgoing general manager Spiro Tsiros knew this moment was the closing of the book for them as well. There were slaps, hugs and kind words while in the corner the man of the hour was performing his last media rites with a stream of interviews.

Stacey Jones had started his first-grade career in suburban Sydney on 23 April 1995. Now, 3779 days later, on 27 August 2005, he provided an exclamation mark to end the last line of his NRL story.

Until then nothing had obviously unsettled him on what had become a farewell tour. He hadn't dropped his emotional guard as the most significant phase of his life came to a close. There was a sense of celebration rather than desolation about him.

But then something happened. Days after that final match the Warriors had their annual awards night; it was always going to be an occasion high on emotion and moderate on elation.

This was the club's time to give thanks for a contribution beyond description. This was a time for one man's closest admirers to, in effect, pay homage. Words weren't needed but they came nonetheless. It was pictures to music that said much, much more; pictures to music that had countless sets of eyes welling up with tears.

To the soundtrack of Five for Fighting's 'Superman', the audience of fellow players, partners and family, management, sponsors, media and more watched the human faces of Stacey Jones not so often seen. It had to tug at the heart strings and it did — except for the man himself. He didn't want to lose it before standing up to speak and he knew he would if he allowed himself to take a peek at the video. So he did what he's been doing his whole sporting life: he tuned out and focused on what he needed to do.

As a footballer he'd learned on playing fields at test level and in the NRL how to control himself and stay in the moment; in farewells he had learned to do just the same.

But then, just when he thought it was safe, Stacey Jones roped himself into another round of farewells, or at least allowed others to rope him in. He accepted the entreaties to once again wear the Kiwi jersey, to round off his time playing the game he values at the highest level with two finals tests against Australia.

And so he set himself up for another night of waving goodbye to rugby league lovers at Sydney's Aussie Stadium and then a reprise performance to his disciples at Ericsson Stadium.

To talk about Stacey Jones is to remember what others have said about him along the way. A year before he played first grade, Gary Prohm, his first coach at senior level, said: 'I have never seen more of a superstar in the making. I have never seen anyone start off in the game with so much ability.'

After just a handful of first-grade appearances, his original Warriors captain Dean Bell offered: 'He has skills, and they're only going to improve, but what he has already, and what sets him apart for one so young, is heart and desire.'

And his one-time team-mate and fellow halfback Greg Alexander put it this way: 'I've seen a lot of kids come into first grade but just two stand out in my mind. I remember Brad Fittler's debut in 1989 and I remember Stacey's in 1995. He made as big an impact as anyone when he came into the game.'

When Stacey Jones finally finished in this part of the world 11 years after that debut, he did so knowing he'd played a total of more than 280 matches for the Kiwis and the Warriors, something like 22,000 minutes spent in battle on fields far and wide. Of the 264 first-grade matches in his club's 11-year history, he played in 238 of them, missed only 18 through injury or being rested and sat on the bench in seven more; and after his Kiwi debut in 1995 he was missing from the New Zealand test side only three times through injury in his country's next 37 internationals.

When it came to records, he owned just about every one on the Warriors' books — most matches, most tries, most points and most field goals. And when awards were handed out he was in a race on his own. In short, he'd dominated the No 7 jersey for club and country like few others have. More than that, he'd dominated the sport period — indeed, he really *was* the game.

As Richard Hadlee is to New Zealand cricket, Stacey Jones is to New Zealand rugby league — a sporting freak, the like of which the country may well never see again.

But it's not goodbye right now. It's au revoir. He'll be back, just not to play again.

Richard Becht
Auckland, September 2005

Statistics

Fact File

Born:	7 May, 1976
Birthplace:	Auckland
Height:	171cm
Weight:	84kg
Representative:	New Zealand 1995–2005
	Junior Kiwis 1994
NRL club:	Warriors 1995–2005
NRL debut:	Warriors v Parramatta, April 23, 1995
Other clubs:	Auckland Vulcans (Lion Red Cup), Point Chevalier, Mount Albert, Ponsonby-Maritime

New Zealand

Tests		Matches	Tries	Goals	FG	Points
1995	v Tonga	1	0	0	0	0
	v Papua New Guinea	1	0	0	0	0
	v Australia	1	0	0	0	0
1996	v Papua New Guinea	2	2	0	0	8
	v Great Britain	3	0	0	0	0
1997	v Australia	2	3	0	0	12
1998	v Australia	3	0	0	0	0
	v Great Britain	3	1	0	1	5
1999	v Australia	2	0	0	0	0
	v Tonga	1	0	0	0	0
2000	v Australia	2	0	0	0	0
	v Lebanon	1	2	6	0	20
	v Wales	1	0	0	0	0
	v France	1	0	0	0	0
	v England	1	0	0	0	0
2001	v France	1	1	0	0	4
	v Australia	1	0	0	0	0
2002	v Australia	1	1	0	0	4
	v Wales	1	1	0	0	4
	v Great Britain	3	2	1	0	10
	v France	1	2	0	0	8
2003	v Australia	1	0	0	0	0
Total		**34**	**15**	**7**	**1**	**75**

Tour Games

		Matches	Tries	Goals	FG	Points
1995	v Resident's XIII	1	0	0	0	0
2002	v St Helens	1	0	0	0	0
	v England A	1	0	0	0	0
Total		**3**	**0**	**0**	**0**	**0**

Test Record – Played 34, Won 21, Drew 2, Lost 11

NB: Test record does not include scheduled appearances in 2005 Tri Nations series. These results were not known at time of publication.

Warriors

	Matches	Tries	Goals	FG	Points
1995	14	5	9	2	40
1996	21	6	0	0	24
1997	18	7	0	1	29
1998	24	6	1	1	27
1999	24	15	5	0	70
2000	19	3	19	0	50
2001	26	10	24	1	89
2002	24	9	6	1	49
2003	22	3	29	4	74
2004	23	6	15	1	55
2005	23	5	63	1	147
Total	**238**	**75**	**171**	**12**	**654**

World Club Challenge

	Matches	Tries	Goals	FG	Points
1997	8	5	0	0	20
Total	8	5	0	0	20

Warriors Record (including WCC): Played 246, Won 118, Drew 3, Lost 125

OVERALL		283	95	178	13	749

Major awards

2005	Rugby League Players' Association — *Best Back Award*
	Warriors — *Life Membership*
2004	Warriors — *Special Award* (200 NRL Games)
2002	Golden Boot — *World's Best Player*
	Halberg Awards — *Finalist Sportsman of the Year*
	New Zealand Rugby League — *Player of the Year*
	New Zealand Rugby League Annual — *Player of the Year*
2001	New Zealand Rugby League — *Player of the Year*
1999	New Zealand Rugby League — *Player of the Year*
	New Zealand Rugby League Annual — *Player of the Year*
	Warriors — *Back of the Year*
	Warriors — *Special Award* (100 NRL Games)
1997	Warriors — *Player of the Year*
	New Zealand Rugby League Annual — *Player of the Year*
1995	Warriors — *Development Player of the Year*
	New Zealand Rugby League Annual — *Promising Player of The Year*